THE MODERN NATIONS IN
HISTORICAL PERSPECTIVE

ROBIN W. WINKS, *General Editor*

The volumes in this series deal with individual nations or groups of closely related nations throughout the world, summarizing the chief historical trends and influences that have contributed to each nation's present-day character, problems, and behavior. Recent data are incorporated with established historical background to achieve a fresh synthesis and original interpretation.

The author of this volume, J. D. LEGGE, is Professor of History at Monash University, Victoria, Australia. He is the author of recent works on regionalism and local government in Indonesia, and also of studies in nineteenth-century British imperial history.

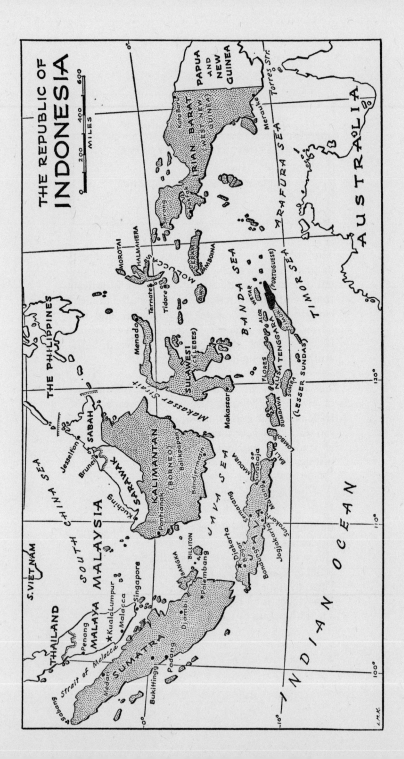

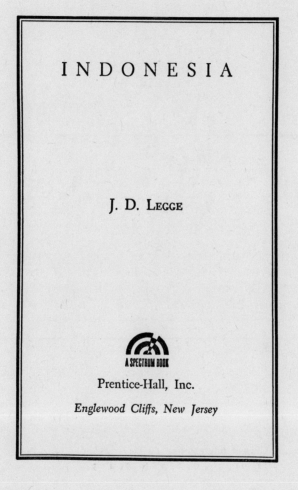

INDONESIA

J. D. LEGGE

A SPECTRUM BOOK

Prentice-Hall, Inc.

Englewood Cliffs, New Jersey

PREFACE

This book is not just a short history of Indonesia, but a commentary upon that history—its character, its main themes, and their contribution to the making of the modern republic. My aim is to call attention to unresolved issues in Indonesian life and to discuss conflicting interpretations of her past development and her present position. I have tried to raise problems, sometimes to suggest answers, and to help the reader pursue further those topics that especially interest him.

I am indebted to my colleagues, Herbert Feith and W. R. Roff, who read the manuscript and offered invaluable criticism; to Mrs. K. Thomson for help in checking sources; to Mrs. P. Leete, Miss R. Swan, and Mrs. V. Cook, who helped at various times with typing; and especially to Mrs. A. V. Morrison, who converted a very messy draft into its neat and final form. I am indebted also to The Free Press of Glencoe, Illinois, for permission to quote from Clifford Geertz, *The Religion of Java* (Copyright © 1960 by The Free Press). Finally, I owe thanks to my Honors class of 1963, who were my unwitting collaborators.

J. D. L.

CONTENTS

vii

ONE

"UNITY IN DIVERSITY"

On August 17, 1945, Indonesia, through the person of Sukarno, declared herself an independent republic. In terms of international law it was to be another four years before formal transfer of sovereignty by the Netherlands established the independent state. But for the modern republic of Indonesia August 17, 1945, remains the important date—an assertion of the fact that Indonesian independence was a matter of right and not of grace. The original declaration was issued in advance of Japanese plans to set up an independent government, for it was not desired to receive independence as a Japanese gift. And the following four years of struggle were to make it clear to the world that the republic was not a gift from the Netherlands either. August 17 was thus to be a symbol of nationalism and of revolutionary origins.

Nationalism and revolution are proud concepts but they do not necessarily carry the same evocative appeal once independence has been gained. In Indonesia's case her nationalism was associated with a belief in liberal-democratic institutions based on Western models —which resulted in part from the Western education enjoyed by many of her nationalist leaders, and in part from the very circumstances of the revolutionary struggle itself, where a devotion to a common goal made possible an easy cooperation between disparate elements. But the parliamentary democracy that came into being in 1949 was not destined to survive in its original form for very long. Subsequent years saw, on the one hand, the development of movements of regional resistance to the center, and on the other a strengthening of central authority. The national unity of the early years of independence began to disappear, and the intellectual elite, which had provided much of the leadership for the prewar nationalist movement as well as for the initial years of the republic, was challenged in its position of predominance by new elements—mass party leaders, the Communist Party, the Army. The end of the first decade of independence found Indonesia engaged in a search for a distinctive political structure and doctrine to replace the Western model she had rejected.

The key to an understanding of these developments must be sought to some extent in a study of the past. First, it is necessary to see the nationalist revolution itself in a wider historical context—in the dramatic terms of the rise and fall of empires, of the emergence of the new republics of Africa and Asia. In many respects Indonesia's experience is not unique but is the product of our age. More narrowly, however, to understand this one particular country, and its present politics, one must examine the deeper currents that have contributed, over the centuries, to the formation of Indonesian society.

These are many and diverse. Her population was formed from the residue of successive migrations that passed through the Indies in their gradual movement from Asia to the open waters of the South Pacific. From an early stage Indonesia was caught up in the pattern of Asia's coastal trade. She was influenced by both India and China, and she still stands balanced between South Asia and the Far East, linked to both but belonging to neither. Also, she accepted Islam. Indonesia may be considered the largest Moslem country in the world, but what has been called "the religion of Java" is a mixture of pre-Hindu animistic beliefs and Hindu survivals as well as of Moslem devotion. The contemporary division between *santri* and *abangan*—between the devout Moslem and the merely nominal Moslem whose real beliefs stem from an older and more accommodating mysticism—reflects the Indonesian ability to absorb differing religious traditions. Again, in terms of social organization, the vestiges of an aristocratic hierarchy still to be observed in modern Indonesia carry echoes of the early Javanese kingdoms. So does the bureaucratic nature of the state. The colonial era, short though it was, was of enormous influence too. In the later years of their East Indian empire, the Dutch welded Indonesia's diverse regions and societies into a more effective political unity than the area had ever before experienced, linked them by a regular, single system of communications, and established the foundations of a new economy. More fundamentally during that period, Indonesia's social patterns were changed and refashioned under contact with Industrial Europe, and many of her more significant characteristics were shaped. But colonial rule did not create modern Indonesia. It provided the environment for nationalism. It helped—and hindered—the formation of a new political unity. Western influences operated within a traditional environment. The nature of the interaction between the two must be a part of our inquiry.

A Diverse Heritage

One of Indonesia's major problems in the modern world is that merely of preserving the unity of the nation. It is not surprising on the face of it that 3,000 islands spread across 3,000 miles of ocean should lack natural cohesion, and it is this fact that leads some observers to argue, and not without plausibility, that modern Indonesia is an artificial creation of the Dutch rather than a reflection of underlying factors binding the archipelago together. The Republic's motto *Bhinneka Tunggal Ika*—unity in diversity—has so far expressed an aspiration rather than a solid reality. There are in fact several senses in which one may speak of unity and diversity. There are, first, the obvious geographical, ethnic, and cultural factors that help make one region similar to, or different from, other regions. Second, there is a striking diversity within the economy of the country: differences between types of economic activity amount almost to the existence of separate economies. Finally, there are the horizontal divisions which affect the social unity of the country. All of these contribute to the complexity of the contemporary scene.

In the first of these senses—the straightforward geographical sense—the country's island character has accentuated regional distinctness but it has also helped to shape the common patterns of traditional society. Between Sabang in northern Sumatra and Merauke in West New Guinea there are many different terrains ranging from the rugged mountain backbone of western Sumatra to the swamps of southern Sumatra and the jungles of Borneo, from the areas of coconut cultivation of Minahasa or of southern Sulawesi to the heavily cultivated rice terraces of Java and Bali. The physical differences between these areas reflect the unevenness of Indonesia's population distribution, and the fact that well over half (approximately 60 million) of the country's population of approximately 100 million is to be found on the island of Java constitutes an extra irritant within the wider problem of regionalism.

These different areas have been the home of distinct societies. In racial terms Indonesia's population is basically of Malay stock, the product of an unknown number of migrations from the Asian mainland pressing on earlier arrivals and driving them inland. Despite this constant ethnological pressure, the long period during which migrations took place (very roughly from 2500 B.C. to 1000 B.C.), the distinction between early and later Malay arrivals in the archipelago, the subsequent admixture of other racial elements, and the comparative isolation of one area of settlement from another have combined to produce many ethnic differences within that common racial framework. It would be difficult to give an exhaustive list of ethnic groups and subgroups in the islands, partly because of the lack of definitive principles of classification. One observer[1] has listed well over a hundred such groups. But fourteen major peoples at least stand out clearly—Atjehnese, Batak, Minangkabau, Coastal Malay, Sundanese, Javanese, Madurese, Balinese, Dyaks, Makassarese, Buginese, Torajas, Menadonese, and Ambonese—and perhaps a few others.[2] These communities, each occupying its own particular region, speaking its own language, and possessing its own forms of social organization, have a sense of distinctness and a local pride that tend in certain circumstances to take precedence over feelings of national loyalty.

The pattern of traditional economic activity varies also. Indonesia's tropical environment, her volcanic soil, and her heavy rainfall have provided hospitality for an intensive agriculture based on an intricate irrigation system, and the terraced hillsides of Java and Bali reflect the perfection of agricultural techniques that have enabled the harvesting in some areas of two crops a year. This type of wet rice cultivation (*sawah*), which, of course, is not unique to Indonesia, is not universal, and a broad economic division may be made between those areas which practice it and those less thickly

[1] Raymond Kennedy, *Bibliography of Indonesian Peoples and Cultures* (Revised edition) ed. T. W. Maretzki and H. T. Fischer (New Haven: Human Relations Area Files, 1955). For an excellent treatment of the ethnic variety of Indonesia, see Hildred Geertz, "Indonesian Cultures and Communities" in Ruth T. McVey (ed.), *Indonesia* (New Haven, 1963).

[2] See, *e.g.*, the list given by W. F. Wertheim, *Indonesian Society in Transition* (The Hague, 1956), p. 25.

populated and more heavily wooded regions which have followed a dry agricultural method based on shifting cultivation (*ladang*). The former represents the type of cultivation in Java and Bali; the latter has formed the more usual method in Sumatra, Borneo, and the eastern islands of the archipelago. While agriculture of either type has formed the basis of a largely subsistence economy, the eastern islands, the Moluccas, have for long produced spices for purposes of trade. And the archipelago has produced its own seafarers while the strategic position of the Indies at the "corner" of Asia has invited the penetration of sailors and traders from further afield.

These ethnic and economic patterns both divide and unite; they underlie the Republic's contemporary problem of regionalism, but together they help to explain some of the dominant themes of Indonesia's history. One of these is the interplay between land and sea—between agricultural societies and commercial societies, between kings and merchants, between Java and the outer islands. The fertility and the consequent intensive agriculture of Java has provided the foundation for the pre-eminent role of that island in the past. Where intensive agriculture prevailed, it was not possible for each village to be a completely closed and selfsufficient unit. Such agriculture required cooperation for the maintenance of the irrigation system on which a series of villages depended. It thus called for some sort of unit to overarch the individual communities. Hence the growth of principalities, supported by agricultural tribute and supplying in return a necessary bureaucratic service. Hence the growth of an ordered society in which rank was important and where it was accompanied by the appropriate material appurtenances, a society in which the court of the prince was not merely a center of government but also of civilization. Indian influences helped to develop and consolidate this political development, elaborating the aristocratic principle and the concept of a divine monarchy with magical powers. In the ebb and flow of Indonesian history principalities became kingdoms and kingdoms empires exercising a unified control over a greater or smaller part of the area.

But against such land-based power was set the power of commerce—both within the archipelago and linking it to the wider trade of eastern and southern Asia; and from the bases of rivers and harbors there developed political authorities dependent upon sea power. The empire of Srivijaya in south Sumatra (from the second half of the seventh century to the thirteenth century) was the greatest of these. The Javanese kingdoms thus had to contend from time to time with the maritime power of commercial empires often based outside Java and possessing a different kind of polity and a different kind of social order.

A second dominant theme in Indonesian history stems from the first—from the character of the interaction between courts and peasantry, between government and the governed. The aristocratic culture of the Indonesian principality rested ultimately upon the village, the principal social unit, grounded in custom and providing something approaching a closed social environment for its inhabitants—a unit which provided a set of norms, a web of rights and obligations. In the case of Java, where the village may be seen most clearly as the basis of a hierarchical order whose other pole was the ruler, the village was essentially a territorial unit. In other parts of Indonesia, ties of kinship in one form or another may form the basis of village organization.[3] But whatever the variations of detail from area to area the village unit, whether the Javanese *desa*, the *negeri* of Minangkabau, or the *marga* of southern Sumatra, has formed the focus of rural life and has embodied the communal values of a peasant culture, distinct from, though in some respects dependent on, the aristocratic world of the prince's court. In Javanese terms the culture of the village is the *abangan* tradition (from the word *abang* meaning elder brother), the communalistic culture of the common people with their shrewdness and their humor, their earthiness and their superstition, as distinct from the more rarefied mores of the *priyayi* or aristocratic class.

These essential elements of a traditional social order are still visible. The Netherlands, in administering Java, inherited the administrative forms of the earlier Javanese kingdoms, and the Dutch government thus helped to preserve the vestiges of a traditional Javanese aristocracy. Confirmed as regents, district officers, or sub-district officers in a European administration, the *priyayi* still retained the authority that was theirs by custom and, in their persons, were able to adapt a traditional pattern of government suited to an agrarian society to the needs of a more complex far-reaching modern administration. At the same time, at the base of society, it was an object of Dutch policy to preserve village society in Java and elsewhere. Paternalistic protection for the village could never completely shut out

---

[3] Barend ter Haar, *Adat Law in Indonesia* (New York, 1948), distinguishes thirteen distinct types of village community.

the solvent influences of colonial rule, but the deep social changes of the last century were still not able to destroy the outlines of a traditional social order. Facile contrasts between custom and innovation, between East and West, between motor car and bullock cart provide the clichés of the travel writer, but even clichés may reflect a certain truth, and the fact remains that the majority of Indonesia's inhabitants are engaged in a peasant agriculture and live within the customary framework of village society.

These observations point to another sense in which one may speak of the problem of unity and diversity within the Indonesian scene. As the Dutch over the course of the last century began to extend their effective control outward from Java and to weld the scattered links of their empire into a clear political and economic unity, the resulting pressures of economic and social change were unevenly felt. In economic terms first of all the investment of Dutch capital in the direct production of plantation products—sugar, tobacco, coffee, tea, rubber, palm oil—or of minerals—tin and oil—gave Indonesia the foundations of a modern economy with its large commercial cities, its import-export houses, its financial institutions. (It is worth noticing how recent a process this was. Indonesians are apt to speak of their 350 years of subjection to Dutch rule without noticing that for the great bulk of this period the interests of the Netherlands were essentially commercial and her actual penetration outside Java slight. It is only with the direct investment of the later years of the nineteenth century that Netherlands India really comes into existence as a closely controlled and developed imperial dependency.) This economic development stood in sharp contrast to peasant cultivation and, in broad terms, it was an alien economy. The big enterprise—whether plantation or banking house or trading concern—was in Dutch hands and, since the corporation was the model, in the hands of shareholders at home rather than in those of independent planters or businessmen in the colony. Small retail trade was predominantly the preserve of the Chinese, who, though not reaching the numerical proportions to which they attained in the Malay Peninsula, nonetheless came to constitute an important element in the populations of Indonesian cities and market towns. Thus foreigners seemed to maintain control of business and commerce, while the Indonesians were left to cultivate the soil.

The Dutch economist, J. H. Boeke, in analyzing the structure of the Netherlands Indian economy, used the term "dual economy" to describe this dichotomy. In Boeke's hands the concept of dualism tended to be used as a central explanatory factor, to be elevated to the level of a general theory in the light of which all features of the Indonesian scene were arranged and interpreted. In this all-embracing sense the term is open to many objections into which it is not necessary to enter fully at this point. For example, too sharp a division must not be made between the two aspects. One has only to observe the intricate pattern of commercial transactions within the depths of rural society, described by one writer in terms of a circulatory system whose arteries "braid out into a complex network of tiny, doubled-over, and marvelously interwound economic capillaries reaching into the small crevices of native life," [4] to see the flourishing existence of an exchange economy below the level of the Chinese-dominated rural market town, and one may doubt whether a separate economic theory is required to deal with the peculiarities of the Indonesian scene. But the concept of a dual economy, if used more loosely, does draw attention to certain obvious features to be observed in Indonesia as well as in her Asian neighbors, where the paraphernalia of large scale business exists side by side with the traditional, labor-intensive economy. The latter's conservatism and apparent imperviousness to change makes for an impression of distinctness between two types of economy.

Accompanying this economic dualism is an analogous dualism of Indonesian society itself—again a phenomenon not confined to Indonesia. The later years of Dutch rule were years of accelerated social change that saw the emergence of a so-called "westernized" elite. This process which Indonesia shared with most other territories under colonial rule, was only in part a deliberate and intentional consequence of Dutch policy. To a great extent it occurred despite policy—it was an inevitable result of more intensive economic penetration and of more thorough and more effective government. But policy did play its part. After 1900 the Netherlands' Ethical Policy, with its concept of a Debt of Honor which had to be repaid to the colony, represented an official attempt to foster as well as to control the direction of social change. The provision of welfare programs in the fields of health, agricultural extension, and education was one aspect of a policy designed to prepare the colony for some kind of self-government, though the exact form this was to take was left vague. Presumably it was intended, at least by some policy makers,

[4] Clifford Geertz, *The Religion of Java* (Illinois, 1960), p. 2.

to develop a relationship between Holland and the Indies along the lines later to be developed between Britain and her former colonies, with some sort of multi racial partnership within the Indies themselves. Some Dutchmen did in fact speak of the development of a new society—"East Indian society"—which was neither Indonesian nor Dutch, but in some way a blend of the two. This idea was never clearly defined and was not, in any case, the sort of goal to be achieved easily. But education and the encouragement of social change presumably fitted into this kind of rationale.

The Ethical Policy was well intentioned and it reflected the general idealism which constituted a not insignificant ingredient in Dutch rule in the Indies. But social change is difficult to control and benevolence in colonial policies often produces the reverse of gratitude. In this case the Netherlands provided education for some Indonesians but failed to provide opportunities for those who received that education. Indonesians were excluded from the higher ranks of government service and in the lower ranks there were far too few openings for those who were qualified. Even in the middle ranks of government service, preference was given to Dutch and Eurasians, and the pressure of their own numbers forced educated Indonesians to accept clerical positions far inferior to their qualifications. The creation of "East Indian society," it would seem, was a very long-term goal and the immediate consequence was the creation of a class of unemployed or underemployed intellectuals. With such discrimination on grounds of race it was not surprising that those whose training had equipped them for leadership should find outlets for their talents in movements of resistance. Holland at one and the same time gave ground for resentment at her domination and provided the training which could organize that resentment into nationalist channels.

In speaking of this development it is necessary to distinguish this emerging westernized elite from Indonesia's traditional elite. As we have noticed, there were class divisions in precolonial society. But these were within the existing culture. The emergence of the modern elite was, by contrast, the product of a contact between widely differing cultures—a contact which had begun, in a variety of ways, to disrupt the existing order. The distinction between the two elites is partly a distinction of function. While Western-educated nationalists were organizing resistance to the Dutch, the Javanese *priyayi* provided the backbone of the territorial administration of the colony.

But it is partly a more subtle distinction of outlook. The *priyayi* remained a part of Javanese society with an outlook on the world distinct from that of the peasantry—more urbane and cultivated, but still within the same world-view. The new elite, on the other hand, was absorbing a Western outlook, and its members often felt more closely tied to European culture than to Indonesia's own heritage. The distinction was not of course an absolute one, but it was, and is, sufficiently clear to be worth emphasis. It represents the Indonesian version of a familiar Asian and African pattern.

The dilemma of the Indonesian intellectuals was given moving expression, in the 1930s, by the man who was later to be prime minister of the struggling republic in the early days of the revolution. "I have been too abstract for my people," wrote Sjahrir[5] from exile, "too far removed from the framework of their concepts, too 'western.' They have been, for me, too inert." [6] Again and again in his letters he returns to the theme of the inertness of the East and the vitality of the West and to the problem this posed for him: "We intellectuals here are much closer to Europe or America than we are to the Baroboedoer or Mahabharata or to the primitive Islamic culture of Java and Sumatra. Which is our basis: the West, or the rudiments of feudal culture that are still to be found in our Eastern society?" [7] Sjahrir's concern was to find some reconciliation between the two. To him the West signified "forceful, dynamic and active life," which he admired despite its "brutality and coarseness." What was needed was some kind of synthesis. "The East must become Western in the sense that it must acquire as great a vitality and dynamism as the West. Faust must reveal himself to the Eastern man and mind. . . ." [8] Sjahrir in exile felt that he had found such a reconciliation: "It was as though I were recalled to my people when I received the banishment sentence." [9] But for others there was a division in the soul that was not easily to be bridged.

Since Indonesia's modern elite had formed the spearhead of the

[5] Soetan Sjahrir, Prime Minister of the Republic of Indonesia from 1945 to 1947 and founder of the Indonesian Socialist Party (PSI). Sjahrir had studied law at Leiden in the early 1930s and had been active in student nationalist circles. After his return to Indonesia in 1932, he engaged in further political activity for which in 1934 he was exiled to Boven Digul in New Guinea where he remained until 1942.

[6] Soetan Sjahrir, *Out of Exile* (New York, 1949), p. 33.

[7] *Ibid.*, p. 27.

[8] *Ibid.*, p. 146.

[9] *Ibid.*, p. 33.

movement of nationalist resistance, it was naturally to this group that the power passed with the transfer of sovereignty. This fact had presented modern Indonesia with certain problems of political authority. If one were called on to focus at one point the various issues of post-independence politics, one could say, with some justice, that they have been concerned in one way or another with the task of maintaining a connection between the groups that together compose the modern elite on the one hand and the mass of the agrarian population on the other, between westernized elements and traditional society, between government and the governed. The new rulers of Indonesia, in effect, inherited a new political entity, and they had to forge an authority based on consent to replace the authority that the Dutch were able to impose in the last analysis by force.

Of particular importance for the future was the fact that the elite, though substantial in absolute terms, was but a tiny fragment of Indonesia's total population. This had important consequences. It meant that independent Indonesia was to be deplorably short of the technical and administrative skills necessary for the running of a modern state. It meant also that there were important, though not necessarily insuperable, difficulties facing the operation of democratic political machinery. At least there was no broadly based middle class to bridge the gulf between the peasant mass and their rulers. Of importance too for Indonesia's future economic development was the fact that the elite was essentially an administrative rather than an entrepreneurial elite.[10] It was to be found in the ranks of government or to a lesser extent in private corporative business and the professions. The great economic expansion produced by Dutch capital investment had not stimulated, and indeed had helped to destroy, an indigenous commercial class. Even under the Dutch East India Company the Dutch endeavor to consolidate its monopoly and to exclude Arab as well as European rivals limited the scope of operations of Javanese merchants. With the subsequent late-nineteenth-century development of the economy there was still little room for the development of an indigenous commercial class.

The unifying effects of colonial rule were thus balanced by its divisive and disruptive effects. The Dutch strengthened certain traditional elements of Indonesian society—the *priyayi* of Java, for example, in becoming the servants of the modern state, were given an

[10] George McT. Kahin, *Nationalism and Revolution in Indonesia* (Ithaca, N.Y., 1952) p. 29.

administrative power which eclipsed that which they had enjoyed traditionally—they created or encouraged the growth of new elements —the Western-educated elite and the Chinese middle-men—and they destroyed others. The resultant amalgam is a society that, in many respects, lacks natural cohesion.

The modern republic in consequence is faced by several types of political problem. Its political leadership forms a tiny proportion of the total population.[11] To bridge the gulf between this elite and the mass of the agrarian population presents a political problem of considerable magnitude whose difficulty may well help to explain any trend toward authoritarianism in post-revolutionary politics. A second problem runs counter to the first. While the narrowness of political leadership may help to make for authoritarian rule, the elite itself has not been a single and unified group, and the divisions within it operate to produce a diffusion rather than a concentration of power. The balance between Moslem, nationalist, and Communist political leadership, between all of them and the power of the Army, the personal power of President Sukarno himself with his revolutionary prestige and his mesmeric oratory, combine to make it difficult for strong leadership to emerge. This diffusion of power is accentuated by a third type of problem—that of strong regional feeling. The local pride of particular regions and ethnic groups helps to foster a suspicion of the central government in Djakarta. As an added element to the problem there is the tension between the Javanese, the numerically dominant ethnic group, and other Indonesians. The traditional interest of the Javanese in government and administration accentuates the fear, in other parts, of Javanese imperialism.

Indonesia's most pressing trouble, in these circumstances is, perhaps, not the danger of personal or minority dictatorship, but the absence of genuine leadership supported by adequate power.

Since Independence: Rivalries and Reversals

An understanding of these general factors helps to throw light on the style of post-revolution politics in Indonesia. Even within the few years since independence, more than one answer has been offered to the country's central problem in the modern world—that of resolving the conflict between tradition and change, of reconciling the interests of a narrow leadership with the conservatism and poverty of Sjahrir's

[11] For a discussion of the term "elite," see Chapter Five.

inert mass. During the revolution and in the early days of the post-revolutionary republic, the goal of the country's leaders, reflecting clearly
a Western outlook, was to create a liberal and democratic regime.

During the actual struggle against the Dutch, the internal political
life of the republic had been based on a series of gentlemen's agreements which were to be of importance in the early years of independence. Just after Sukarno had proclaimed Indonesian independence in
August 1945 a "Central Indonesian National Committee" was formed
by the leaders of the nationalist movement to represent the main
political forces in the country. This committee served for the next few
years, while the republic was fighting for its life, as a substitute for a
national parliament. In the absence of any possibility of elections, the
members of this *ad hoc* body were appointed by the President, but
in such a manner that they did genuinely include the various strands
of revolutionary opinion and interest. Though appointive, it was a
representative body whose members enjoyed real support and whose
character commanded a general acceptance. The second gentlemen's
agreement concerned the original constitution of the republic whose
drafting was hastily completed after the proclamation. It was a presidential constitution designed to place considerable power in Sukarno's
own hands. But in the early weeks of its existence pressure made itself
felt within the Central National Committee for the formation of
cabinets responsible to the committee rather than to the president.
Sukarno accepted this pressure, and without any constitutional
amendment allowed the Constitution of 1945 to operate as though
it in fact provided for a parliamentary system with responsible government.

Independence was thus launched in a way that appeared to encourage, or at least to allow the possibility of, the rapid growth of
liberal democratic conventions. The circumstances of the struggle
with Holland helped to create and preserve a considerable degree of
cooperation among nationalist leaders such as to promote the operation of these conventions. At the same time there was a wide agreement among those leaders as to fundamental aims. With the final
transfer of sovereignty to Indonesia in 1949, there were grounds for
expecting the smooth development of a republic whose main outlines
were democratic in a Western tradition. Sovereignty was actually
transferred to a federal state, the Republic of the United States of
Indonesia (RUSI), whose constitution was designed to recognize, and
cater to, the existence of regional feeling. Within a year republican

suspicion of the federal principle as being a Dutch-inspired device
led to the replacement of the provisional federal constitution by a
unitary constitution. The latter, however, preserved the parliamentary
forms and the idea of responsible government, and it appeared not to
affect the expectation of a democratic regime on Western lines and
operated by individuals whose education had rendered them to a
great extent Western in outlook.

The expectation was to be comparatively short-lived. In spite of the
fact that the year 1955 saw the successful holding of national elections for a new parliament to replace the appointive, *ad hoc*, parliament (the result of another gentlemen's agreement), there were already apparent the signs of a shifting domestic balance of power
which was to be less favorable to the preservation of a democratic
system. The emergence of divisions within the intellectual elite, the
change in the character of political leadership consequent upon the
development of the mass party, the unobstrusive recovery of the Indonesian Communist Party, the uncertain but increasingly assertive role
of the Army—all helped to change the balance of forces within which
Indonesia's parliamentary institutions were operating. The elections
themselves, though overwhelmingly successful as a political experiment, revealed the character of some of these changes. They practically eliminated the Socialist Party, the party that had provided
much of the intellectual leadership of the early years of the Republic,
and revealed an increase in the comparative strength of the Java-based
parties, the Nationalist Party (PNI), the Moslem Teachers Party,
Nahdatul Ulama (NU) and the Communist Party (PKI), as against
the other major Moslem party, the Masjumi, which drew the bulk
of its support from outside Java.

The next five years saw the gradual rejection of the political forms
with which Indonesia had embarked upon her career of independence,
and the accompanying attempt to replace the political ideas on which
those forms were based by others supposedly derived from the republic's own inner "identity." In 1957 Sukarno announced to the nation
that liberal democracy on the Western model had failed to meet the
particular needs of Indonesia and he called upon it to fashion a specifically Indonesian form of democracy—a democracy with leadership
rather than the "fifty per cent plus one" type of democracy of the
West. In particular he wanted political procedures to follow what he
believed to be the model of the village, where questions were talked
out until a general consensus was achieved. Deliberation and con-

sensus—*musjawarah* and *mufakat*—were to be the essential principles of "guided democracy."

In practical terms the ideas of deliberation and consensus required, in Sukarno's eyes, the formation of a government that represented all the main political parties, *i.e.*, a government that included representatives of the Communist Party. He wanted also to see the establishment of a council comprised, not simply of party representatives, but of representatives of what he called "functional groups"—peasants, workers, youth, religious groups, the various regions of the country, and so forth. Such a council would represent the nation more genuinely than did a parliament composed merely of party representatives, and its discussions would therefore enable a genuine national consensus to emerge. Sukarno's plan was not formulated in very clear terms, but the suggestion of a four-party government including the Communist Party evoked firm resistance, particularly from the outer islands. In East Indonesia, Borneo, South Sumatra, and Atjeh military commanders assumed control of the administration in their respective areas. The government resigned and a state of emergency was declared.

The new government that was formed was in theory a nonparty government though it did have party representatives within it, including two Communist-sympathizers. It was not, however, the kind of four-party coalition that the President apparently had desired. A National Council was formed, representing the various interests of the country, but it was an advisory body only and it lacked the authority that Sukarno had hoped it would exercise.

These political changes of 1957 were followed, after a period of uncertainty, by open revolt in Sumatra and North Sulawesi in February 1958. The revolt was suppressed more easily than many observers had expected, but the events of 1957 and 1958 had, nonetheless, changed beyond recognition the power structure with which Indonesia had embarked on her career as an independent republic. The power and prestige of the Army had been greatly enhanced by its success in dealing with the revolt. The President had strengthened his own position as a result of his direct intervention in politics. The power of the parties had declined. A new constellation of forces had emerged, and the way was open for the President to secure a formal rejection of "liberal democracy" and the introduction of his "guided democracy." The most important single step toward his goal was his decision in July 1959 to decree a return to the Constitution of 1945. By contrast with the provisional Constitution of 1950, the Constitution of 1945 was extraordinarily flexible and open in its prescriptions. It prescribed no formal checks on the exercise of presidential authority. It created no framework for the institutionalizing of political behavior. In externals it appeared to establish something approaching a personal dictatorship.

This would be a misleading judgment. Sukarno's powers under the Constitution were extensive, but he was nonetheless bound by the political circumstances of any given time. He, too, had to win support, to feel his way, to bargain, to negotiate, and his power was much more circumscribed than the Constitution itself would have suggested. The operation of guided democracy depended upon a shifting alignment of forces in which, for the time being, the relations of President and Army constituted the most constant factor. After 1959 power was, in effect, shared between the two, though in varying proportions.

These developments will be described more fully below.[12] Though Sukarno, it is true, did not become a dictator as a result of the return to the Constitution of 1945, nonetheless, Indonesian political life has acquired a more authoritarian flavor since then. Control of the press and detention of some of the opponents of the regime are important signs of this. So is the attempt to fashion a new political orthodoxy, reflected in the government's use of slogans and symbols as a means of rallying support for the regime. The background to these developments has been a continuing economic crisis. There has been a catastrophic decline in foreign reserves and a continuing inflation, but no serious attempt has been made to come to grips with economic problems. Rather the emphasis has been on spectacular demonstrations of Indonesia's prestige—the Asian Games or the Games of the New Emerging Forces, for instance—and upon an adventurous foreign policy focused first on West New Guinea and then upon the newly formed Federation of Malaysia. The trend of events by the early 1960s had become set in a direction contrary to that of the early days of Indonesian independence.

Unresolved Issues

In surveying the first years of independence, there is a danger that too close a view may either obscure the main trend of events or may tempt one to too facile an account of them. Superficially Indonesia's record is not a particularly unusual one. Nationalism, independence,

[12] See Chapter Seven.

a hopeful democratic beginning, crisis, and the decline of liberal institutions, the increase in Presidential and Army power—these steps echo those of other emergent states. A closer examination of the Indonesian case, however, reveals peculiarities of pattern that distinguish her in greater or lesser degree from her neighbors. Her geographical diversity poses obvious and very special problems as does her ethnic diversity. Her density of population and the consequent unfavorable ratio between resources and numbers confronts her with an economic task of exceptional magnitude, and her ability to handle it is affected by the dichotomy, previously discussed, between an almost subsistence economy and an export economy. This dichotomy may not be peculiar to her, but it is unusually sharp in her case. She lacks a strong native entrepreneurial class, and though there remain the vestiges of an administrative system appropriate to a purely agrarian society, she lacks also a reserve of trained technicians and administrators educated for the needs of a commercial age.

Within this framework Indonesia's political forces were in process of defining themselves during the first years of independence. Politics, even in the early years, has not been a conflict between clearly articulated programs. Major differences of policy did exist, certainly—Was a federal structure really less desirable than a unitary structure? Was Indonesia to be an Islamic state or not? What was to be the role of foreign capital in economic development? And for some of these issues there have been exponents of a coherent enough point of view. The West Java Masjumi leader Isa Anshary, for instance, was single-minded in his advocacy of an Islamic state. Sukarno himself, with his attempt to fashion a distinctively Indonesian point of view from such diverse sources as Marx and Marhaen,[13] was certainly as concerned with political ideas as he was later in his advocacy of guided democracy. But the ideas of these leaders did not reflect the essence of the Indonesian political struggle, and the events of the 1950s cannot be given a simple interpretation in such ideological terms. In terms of organized groups, the main alignment of opposing forces, after the shifting Masjumi–PNI relationship of the pre-election years, was that

[13] Marhaen was the name of a peasant whom Sukarno took as a symbol for "the destitute People of Indonesia." As a peasant who did not live by selling his labor, he could not be described as a proletarian. Sukarno, by taking him as a symbol, was seeking to develop a social philosophy applicable, in particular, to a poor peasantry. See his lecture of July 1957 to the 30th anniversary meeting of the PNI, where this theme was developed: *Marhaen and Proletarian* (Cornell Modern Indonesia Project, Translation Series, Ithaca, 1960).

between Sukarno and his supporters on the one hand and Masjumi and PSI on the other. But again this division was cut across by so many other issues that it does not stand out in such a way as to serve as a guide to the intricacies of Indonesia's political life. With the establishment of a government dominated by President and Army, effective opposition was crushed. But the diffusion of real power within the country remained, a reflection of elitist politics and regionalism. As a general judgment it can be said that, even by the end of the first decade, there was still no very clear *structure* of political activity, no firmly established *procedures* and *conventions*. These were still to be determined, if they were to be determined at all, in practice, in the actual interplay of day-to-day affairs.

The explanation of these inadequacies is complex. Liberal democracy failed in part because it lacked any real defenders and in part because it simply could not deliver the goods. Given the uneven development of the economy, the heavy dependence on export markets, and, in general, the unfavorable ratio between resources and population, no regime could have fulfilled popular expectations, and in those circumstances other divisions that were part of Indonesia's total situation—a product of her history and of more recent circumstances—were enabled to assert themselves. Open party competition itself encouraged particular interests to make a vigorous assertion of their demands. To explain these developments one must point to those aspects of colonial rule that created the modern Indonesian elite and gave it its distinctive character. Of particular importance is the fact that the elite was an administrative rather than an entrepreneurial middle class. Here lies, in part, the reason for the type of rivalries that have emerged within the elite since independence, and for the general increase in bureaucratic power in modern Indonesia. One must point also to the basic fact that Indonesia, before the arrival of the Dutch, had never had a tight unity. And one must notice the characteristics of traditional society—in particular the hierarchical tradition of an agrarian order that has made but an uneasy adjustment to the needs of a commercial age.

Indonesian history itself reflects many of these themes. The conflict between Java and the outer islands is of long standing. At one time it may be seen as a conflict between the maritime empire of Srivijaya in southern Sumatra and the land-based kingdoms of Java. The same conflict in another form is repeated when the maritime empire of the Dutch comes into contact with the remnants of the

Moslem kingdom of Mataram. This is again the conflict between kings and merchants. It may also, perhaps, underlie the conflict between guided democracy and liberal democracy. But in looking at the recent and the more distant past one becomes aware also of conflicts at another level—conflicts in the soul between old forms and new realities, between traditional views of the world and novel ones. These conflicts may focus in the one man the main elements of Indonesia's contemporary crisis.

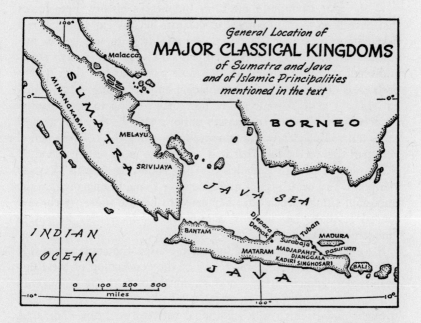

General Location of
MAJOR CLASSICAL KINGDOMS
of Sumatra and Java
and of Islamic Principalities
mentioned in the text

TWO

HINDU INFLUENCES

THE EARLY KINGDOMS

An attempt to sift from Indonesia's history those forces that have been most important in creating her present situation is a risky enterprise. Enough has been said already in these pages to suggest the importance of the colonial period. The Dutch in their three-and-a-half centuries of contact, but more particularly in their eighty-or-so years of genuine and all-embracing empire, changed traditional patterns. In at least some senses they may be said to have created artificially the modern Indonesian nation, with its divisions as well as its unity. But clearly the temptation to stress the colonial period is in part due to the fact that it is merely the most recent period. It is also due in part to a tendency to see Indonesia from a Western viewpoint, and, which is not quite the same thing, to imagine that the important things which have happened to her are those which have tended to make her more Western—those which have helped to "modernize" her.

It would indeed seem hard to overemphasize the consequences, in political, social and economic terms, of the penetration of the European trader, soldier, investor, and administrator from the seventeenth century onwards. But clearly, whatever transformations may have been wrought under Dutch rule, traditional patterns were not eliminated. The degree to which they persisted and were able to assimilate external influences, the degree to which they were modified, or the degree to which they were submerged, is a question of fine judgment. Or rather Western influences and traditional configurations have become so completely interwoven that any attempt to sort them out faces al-

most overwhelming difficulties. But at least it is quite clear that fundamental features of traditional patterns have survived. In Indonesia
as in other Asian countries, societies have existed not merely in their
relation to the West; they have a history of their own in which the
Western impact is but a part and, for the bulk of that period of contact, not the most important part.

This problem of perspective has worried historians in recent years.
They have become sensitive to the effect that their general point of
view and, in particular, their own cultural environment might have
on their handling of Asian history, whether in leading them to apply
a Western set of values, or in persuading them to overemphasize the
historical role of the West. The problem is not confined to Western
historians: Asian historians themselves, while rejecting the value judgments of their Western colleagues, still tend to accept their categories
of historical judgment.[1]

A classic criticism of the Europe-centric approach to Asian history
has been that of the Dutch scholar, J. C. van Leur, whose studies of
the organization of early Indonesian trade have helped to give a new
direction to the study of Indonesian history.[2] In graphic terms he
complained that, though the earlier periods of Indonesian history
might often have been treated by European historians as having an
autonomy of their own, the later centuries have not been: ". . . with
the arrival of ships from Western Europe, the point of view is turned
a hundred and eighty degrees and from then on the Indies are observed from the deck of the ship, the ramparts of the fortress, the high
gallery of the trading house." [3] Van Leur's criticism applies at a vari-

---

[1] See, e.g., K. M. Panikkar, Asia and Western Dominance (London, 1953),
which elaborates the concept of an "age of Vasco de Gama," and in general accepts the idea that the coming of the European was a watershed. In the case of
Western historians, notice that even those who are particularly sensitive to the
autonomy of Asian history may tend to place particular emphasis upon the European period. E.g., D. G. E. Hall, in A History of South-East Asia (London, 1955),
entitled his opening section "The Pre-European Period." His remaining subdivisions—"South-East Asia During the Earlier Phase of European Expansion,"
"The Period of European Territorial Expansion," and "Nationalism and the
Challenge to European Domination" suggest that the history of the area may
be told largely in terms of European challenge and Asian response. The revised
edition, London 1964, entitles the first subdivision "To the Beginning of the
Sixteenth Century." See Hall's own discussion of the question: "On the Study
of Southeast Asian History," Pacific Affairs, September 1960.

[2] See his essays published in English under the general title Indonesian Trade
and Society (The Hague, 1955).

[3] Ibid., p. 261.

ety of levels.[4] It can refer to the making of judgments of value. In the modern period in particular there is a danger of bias in one direction or the other in the assessment of European imperialism. It can refer to the historian's angle of vision—the eyes through which the events are seen. Again for the colonial period the fact that the most easily accessible sources are the records of the colonizers themselves, creates the special danger that events will be seen from their standpoint. Or it can refer to the historian's judgment of which factors have been most important in shaping the course of events. This third sense is perhaps the most important and the most difficult to resolve, though the three meanings are, of course, interconnected. If events are seen from the point of view of the European (in the sense of through his eyes) there will be a natural tendency for the historian to judge in terms of Western standards, and also to see the influence of Europeans as having been decisive in determining the course of events.[5]

Van Leur himself seems to have been concerned with all of the senses in which the terms "Europe-centric" and "Asia-centric" could be used, but it was perhaps the third with which he was most preoccupied. He was concerned to argue that, while the European impact on Asia was important, it could not be regarded as a single phenomenon, and its real importance was limited to merely a part of the period of European contact. In his view the Europeans, during their early years of commercial penetration, were essentially peripheral to Indonesian history. Long before the sixteenth century Indonesia already played an integral part in Asian coastal trade whose trade routes extended from the Middle East to China. In van Leur's terminology it was a peddling trade, based not on the activities of an entrepreneurial middle class but on investment in individual voyages by princes or members of an aristocratic class, and actually carried on by peddlers, who merely collected and carried the products of handicraft industry, or garden products such as pepper, cloves, and other

[4] The fullest exploration of the various levels, and of the whole problem of perspective in the writing of Asian history, is given by John Smail, "On the Possibility of an Autonomous History of Modern Southeast Asia," *Journal Southeast Asian History*, Vol. II, No. 2 (July 1961). For a fuller discussion of Smail's argument, see Chapter Four. For a different point of view, see John Bastin, *The Western Element in Modern Southeast Asian History* (Papers on Southeast Asian Subjects, No. 2, Department of History, The University of Malaya, Kuala Lumpur, 1960).

[5] But note, for example, Panikkar, whose moral viewpoint is Asia-centric, but whose judgment of historical significance still tends to place the European in the center of the picture.

spices. With the coming of the Portuguese, and later the Dutch and the English, the patterns of this trade were not at first essentially altered. The Europeans, rather, fitted into existing patterns; their trading companies were in effect merchant princes, whose agents were peddlers, albeit on a larger scale; they avoided territorial responsibilities and made only a minor impact upon the society of the Indies.[6] As Smail points out,[7] the increase of Dutch power in the eighteenth century made van Leur uncertain of the continuing autonomy of Indonesian history, and he seems to have accepted the idea that in the nineteenth century the impact of the West was more significant than the forces of the society on which the impact was made—"the autonomous, indigenous order of things." [8] Nonetheless, for the main course of Indonesian history, he argues that, though various foreign cultures have exerted their influence, they did not change fundamentally Indonesia's social and political order. "The sheen of the world religions and foreign cultural forms is a thin and flaking glaze; underneath it the whole of the old indigenous forms has continued to exist." [9] The validity of this general argument will need to be examined more closely at a later point in this essay.[10] At this point it is enough to say, in broad terms, that van Leur's battle has been won. There is no opposition in principle to the necessity of avoiding a Europe-centric view of Asian history if by that is meant the importation of European values to a situation where they do not apply, nor to the view that Indonesian history should not merely be seen over the shoulder of the European. Nor would it be disputed that, even during the period of deepest colonial penetration, the broad outlines of traditional culture survived.

But while these points would be admitted, it should also be recognized that the antithesis between "traditional" society and the changes effected under Dutch rule is in important respects a false one.

[6] The main statement of van Leur's thesis is to be found in his essay "On Early Asian Trade" in *Indonesian Trade and Society*. For a thorough discussion and reassessment of the details of his argument see M. A. P. Meilink-Roelofsz, *Asian Trade and European Influence in the Indonesian Archipelago between 1500 and about 1630* (The Hague, 1962). See also D. K. Bassett, "European Influence in South-East Asia, c. 1500-1630," *Journal Southeast Asian History*, Vol. 4, No. 2 (September 1963).

[7] *Loc. cit.*

[8] Van Leur, "On Early Asian Trade," p. 96.

[9] *Ibid.*, p. 95.

[10] For a consideration of this and other aspects of van Leur's general theory, see Chapter Four.

In the first place, so-called "traditional" society itself has been the product of many influences, some of them external influences operating over a very long period of time. And in the second place it is misleading to speak of *a* traditional society as though it were a simple homogeneous thing. There is not one tradition but many. In Java alone it is customary to notice three distinct types of ingredient in the ideological pattern—the survival of elements of age-old animism, the presence of elements of a Hindu conception of the universe, and the more obvious strength of Islam. One observer has found it convenient to link these traditional views of the world with the village, the government, and the market place respectively.[11] The Javanese village, with its social views emphasizing harmony and cooperation, is "as old as the Javanese" and its syncretic mixture of animistic belief overlaid by Hinduism and Islam all go to form the *abangan* tradition. The market place has been associated with a purer form of Islam, that of the devout *santri*. In the field of government the vestiges of a Javanese aristocracy, the *priyayi*, stemming from the old Javanese kingdoms, but taken over and used and preserved by the Dutch, provided a highly sophisticated, highly civilized, hierarchical, and mystical view of the world, which frequently remains an important constituent of the outlook even of the Westernized civil servant of the later colonial period and of the modern republic.

These three traditions should not be too sharply distinguished from one another, and the correlation made between the *abangan* view and the village, the *santri* view and the market, and the *priyayi* and the world of government and administration is an extremely general correlation only. The presence of Islamic constituents in the *abangan* way of life has been mentioned, and the village itself in greater or lesser degree, even in Java has its *santri*. The same man may at one time be calculating favorable auspices according to the Javanese numerological system, and at another be observing the Moslem month of fasting. There are villages that, as a whole, are more devout than their neighbors, and within any one village there are devout individuals and others whose belief is worn more lightly. In some cases the *abangan–santri* division is one of open opposition, but even *abangan* ritual has its Islamic elements. Similarly Indian influence is not confined to the aristocratic culture of the *priyayi*. Though only in Bali is Hinduism to be found as an active religion, the evidence of the *wayang* stories drawn from the *Ramayana* and *Mahabharata* are but

[11] Clifford Geertz, *The Religion of Java* (Illinois, 1960).

one sign of Indian influence upon the culture of the village. However the three world views of *abangan, santri,* and *priyayi* are distinct enough to illustrate the variety and also the complexity of the Indonesian scene and to stress the danger of speaking too easily of *a* traditional way of life, an "autonomous, indigenous order of things." There are many traditions, including other than Javanese traditions, having their roots deep in the past and compounded of imported as well as indigenous influences.

There is still a third objection to the "traditional–modern" antithesis. We must recognize not merely the complexity of the cultural heritage that has survived, but also the fact that traditional society has itself not remained static—a melange of customary folkways that can stand in contrast to later "westernized" society. Over the centuries before the coming of the European, changes occurred in agricultural techniques, in social organization, in religious belief. To mention but one example, we will have occasion later in these pages to notice the growing complexity of Javanese wet rice cultivation as population grew. And even the westernization of the later years of Dutch empire did not stand in simple opposition to an old order. It was mixed up with it. Change took place within the existing mold or framework, and the new twentieth century Western-educated elite retained many elements of older ways of thought.

This argument could be extended a good deal further, but enough has been said to cast doubts on too glib a reference to tradition and change, and to suggest that any antithesis between the two must be largely a manner of speaking. In any society with an extended history there is bound to be both change and sustained identity. The continuity of Chinese history is a byword; but there is no quantitative way of determining whether the historian should stress its unchanging character or whether he should emphasize the developments that did occur over the centuries to make Ch'ing China very different from T'ang China. The same point applies to Indonesia where, superficially at least, there appear to have been more revolutionary changes over the last thousand or fifteen hundred years. Whether one stresses innovation or continuity must depend in part on the specific point one wishes to make and upon the context within which it is to be made. There is no abstract answer to be given.

While recognizing the complexity of the Indonesian cultural scene it is still worthwhile attempting to disentangle the main elements in the picture, and at least considering whether it is possible to determine the relative importance of the external and indigenous influences in change. Van Leur is not alone in his conviction that, in spite of the pressures from the outside world, Indonesian culture has preserved its identity. D. G. E. Hall makes a similar point when, in speaking of early Indonesian history, he warns against "the insidious tendency to overstress the part played by the imported cultures and to underrate the importance of the indigenous ones of the area." [12] For other scholars, too, village conservatism, the survival within it of ancient belief and custom, and its firmly settled economic patterns have encouraged the view that traditional society is comparatively stable and unchanging. For Schrieke "the Java of around 1700 A.D. was in reality the same as the Java of around 700 A.D." [13] At the same time, and in spite of this impressive unanimity of opinion, there is a danger that one may lean over too far backwards. Are the foreign influences really no more than a thin, flaking glaze?

The Hinduized Kingdoms

Are foreign influences a thin, flaking glaze? This sort of question is of importance first for a consideration of those features of Indonesia's social order which derived from the early Javanese kingdoms—the "Hindu-Javanese kingdoms" as they are called.[14] The wealth of Javanese architectural remains have testified so effectively to the power and organizational complexity of these states that the temptation to read the early history of Indonesia in terms of Indian influence is a powerful one. Apart from material remains, the consequences of India's impact are to be seen in the significance of the concept of kingship in the Javanese principalities and in the survival of the aristocratic administrative system to which reference has already been made. And in rural society the popularity of the shadow plays based on Indian epic themes, the form of Javanese and Balinese dances,

[12] Hall, *op. cit.*, p. 4.

[13] B. J. O. Schrieke, "Ruler and Realm in Early Java," in *Indonesian Sociological Studies: Selected Writings of B. Schrieke*, Vol. II (The Hague, 1957), p. 100. For a criticism of the emphasis on continuity see J. M. van der Kroef, "On the Writing of Indonesian History," *Pacific Affairs*, Vol. XXXI, No. 4 (December 1958). For a specific criticism of Schrieke's dictum, see Harry J. Benda, "The Structure of Southeast Asian History: Some Preliminary Observations," *Journal Southeast Asian History*, Vol. 3, No. 1 (March 1962).

[14] The term "Hindu-Javanese" itself is misleading since Buddhist influence has been of enormous importance too. The term "Hindu" has been used nonetheless, not merely with reference to Indonesia, but in respect to Indian influence in Southeast Asia as a whole. See, for example, the title of George Coedès' book *Histoire ancienne des états hindouisés d'Extrème-Orient* (Hanoi, 1944).

the use of Indian motifs in the traditional *batik* designs[15] all combine to present a picture of strong Indian influence over the best part of a thousand years from approximately the fifth to the fifteenth century.

Such cultural pressures could not suddenly create a new society. It is, of course, not easy to determine quite what level Indonesian development had reached before the reception of Indian influence. Inquiries into social origins must inevitably involve a good deal of speculation. Are there regular stages through which primitive societies pass on their way to a higher material culture and more complex forms of political and social organization? Does a hunting and food gathering economy gradually acquire the techniques of shifting agriculture and then in time learn the practice of a sedentary agriculture? How are the major technological innovations seized upon? These are exciting questions[16] but are no easier to answer in Indonesia than elsewhere, and one can only reconstruct in broad outline the sort of thing that must have happened. Before Indian cultural influences made themselves felt, Indonesians, in parts of Java at least, had devised techniques of irrigation, domesticated the water buffalo, and developed the outlines of a sedentary agriculture. These economic developments had replaced, presumably, some form of shifting cultivation, and they represented a considerable technological revolution. This revolution fashioned the Javanese landscape—a landscape which, in Schrieke's words, was then able "to retain its dominating influence through the ages." [17] The economic revolution must, in turn, have been accompanied by the growth of political units of some size and complexity as a limited chieftainship, based on small groups of families, gave way perhaps first to a tribal pattern of authority and later to a political system in which strong leadership, supported by an elite, had become more clearly defined. But the details of these processes are unknown. The mists clear and history begins to have a slightly solider foundation only after the first signs of Indian influence appear about the beginning of the fifth century. By the seventh century A.D. the main outlines of the characteristic political situation of the is-

[15] Frits A. Wagner, *Indonesia*, "Art of the World" Series, Vol. II (London, 1959).
[16] Anthropologists in the past have tended to shy away from speculation about social origins, but, even in the absence of firm evidence, such questions are legitimate. See, *e.g.*, Robert Redfield, *The Primitive World and Its Transformations* (Ithaca, N.Y., 1953).
[17] B. J. O. Schrieke, *Ruler and Realm, loc. cit.*, p. 100.

lands may be discerned—a situation in which a varying number of kingdoms rival one another, conquer and absorb one another, and contribute to new groupings as dynasties rise or fall or merge. These kingdoms reveal themselves as powerful—how powerful may be a matter of doubt—but at least they must have been complex in organization, and able to control mass labor and to mobilize considerable military or naval force.

The first major example of these developments was the rise of the kingdom of Srivijaya based on southern Sumatra, a center of Hinayana Buddhism, which held sway from about the seventh to the thirteenth centuries. Srivijaya's power was maritime in character, and though it was the dominant power in the area and able to establish control over the harbors of its potential competitors in much of western Indonesia and the Malay Peninsula, it left no material evidences of civilization to compare, for example, with the roughly contemporary Borobodur stupa and the Prambanan complex of temples in central Java. And in spite of Srivijaya's period of pre-eminence the center of political gravity in Indonesia was indeed to be found for the most part on the island of Java. Here a series of major kingdoms, at first in central Java and then in the eastern part of the island, marked the growth of a sophisticated material culture, and of a political strength which, after fluctuations and divisions, reached its apex with the rise of the kingdom of Madjapahit in the thirteenth century.

The first of these Hindu-Javanese kingdoms, Mataram, under the rule of King Sanjaya, flourished in central Java at the beginning of the eighth century. It was Shivaistic in religion and it has left some of the earliest of Java's temple remains on the Dieng Plateau of central Java (an area, incidentally, that is regarded as having already been a sacred area to the Javanese before the days of Indian influence). Sanjaya's Hindu kingdom was followed by a Buddhist interlude under the Shailendra dynasty, which produced perhaps the greatest of all of Indonesia's temple monuments, the Borobodur, and which may have extended power over Srivijaya itself. Shailendra rule in Java was comparatively brief and in the mid-ninth century it was replaced by the new Hindu kingdom of Mataram, claiming to be a restoration of Sanjaya's kingdom. The Shailendras continued as rulers of Srivijaya.

At this point it is necessary to make an important distinction between two types of polity that could be observed in Indonesia's Hinduized kingdoms. On the one hand the Javanese states were inland kingdoms, based on wet rice cultivation, or rather on tribute drawn from it, and displaying a complex hierarchical administrative organization. They were aristocratic and military in character. The court of the ruler reflected the complexity of the political order and the splendor of a distinctive civilization. It was the center of the kingdom, the residence of the principal functionaries of the state, the storehouse of wealth, the headquarters of a powerful military establishment, and the source, in general, from which authority radiated. It was also the cultural and religious center of the kingdom. Between the city and the village the links were maintained by an elaborate pyramidal structure. Local chiefs, brought under central control, were transformed in time into a class of aristocratic officials of the kingdom. In the last analysis royal power depended on the rice, which, in the form of tribute, could maintain a military machine and the administrative apparatus necessary to the service of the royal city. And the control of rice, or of the labor that produced it, was buttressed by the magico-religious character of the monarchy itself.

In contrast to the land-based power of the Javanese kingdoms, stood the maritime power of the commercial states. Srivijaya was the supreme example of this type of polity, but the harbors of the north coast of Java also saw the growth of smaller principalities that drew their strength from trade, which were strong enough to maintain their independence against the inland kingdoms for extended periods. Dependent upon international trade routes, the maritime principalities were cosmopolitan in character and of necessity demonstrated a degree of social equality and tolerance that contrasted sharply with the hierarchy of the land-based kingdoms. A fluctuating tension between the two types complicated the dynastic rivalries of the Javanese kingdoms themselves, and the conflict between Srivijaya and Mataram, for example, illustrates a familiar theme in Indonesian history—the conflict between a land-based *sawah* economy and the different polity of a commercial kingdom.

It is not necessary here to trace in detail the political history of Indonesia during the period of Hindu influence, for this story is told elsewhere.[18] With the fall of Mataram, a consequence of its conflict with Srivijaya, power shifted to eastern Java under the rule of the

[18] For a brief summary of the main stages, see B. H. M. Vlekke, *Nusantara* (Cambridge, Mass., 1944; revised edition, The Hague, 1959), Chs. 1-3; or D. G. E. Hall, *History of Southeast Asia*, Chs. 3 and 4.

semilegendary figure of Airlangga. After establishing his power over a large part of Java, Airlangga divided his kingdom between his two sons and he himself retired to a life of monastic contemplation. The successor kingdoms of Kadiri and Djanggala were in due course reunited under Ken Angrok who had usurped the throne of Djanggala, and who founded the dynasty of Singhosari. Singhosari, during the thirteenth century, expanded its power and under Kertanegara again laid the foundations of an extensive empire. Internal revolt combined with pressure from the Mongol dynasty of China brought Kertanegara's reign to an end in 1292, but his son-in-law, Widjaya, after temporizing with the Chinese invaders, and using them to support his own bid for the throne, was then in a position to exploit them and and to establish the new kingdom of Madjapahit, the last and the greatest kingdom of the Hindu-Javanese period.[19] During the fourteenth century under the direction of King Hayam Wuruk's Chief Minister, Gadjah Mada, Madjapahit claimed suzerainty over the whole archipelago. This power did not last; the penetration of Islam hastened the gradual distintegration of the kingdom, though it did not disappear entirely until the early sixteenth century.

These are merely the main signposts. It is perhaps worth digressing for a moment to touch upon the problem of the historicity of the events of this whole period. What are the sources on which the story depends and how sound is our knowledge of it? These are questions that have greatly concerned scholars in recent years. For the earlier period the story must be pieced together from odd pieces of epigraphical evidence together with occasional references in Chinese chronicles.[20] Not until the fourteenth century is literary evidence available. The *Nagarakertagama*, an epic by Hayam Wuruk's court poet, Prapantja, gives an account of Javanese history from the foundation of Singhosari.[21] It appears to have been based on an early chronicle, the *Pararaton*, though our knowledge of the latter comes only from

[19] Schrieke suggests a geographical interpretation of the ebb and flow of these wars. Java was composed of a conglomeration of distinct geographical regions that contributed a "natural source of disintegration." Because of this, "periodical dismemberment was inherent in the character of the realm." *Ruler and Realm*, p. 100.

[20] Hall, *op. cit.*, gives an indication of the sort of light thrown by these.

[21] For a new translation of the epic, see Theodore G. Th. Pigeaud (trans.), *Java in the 14th Century, a Study in Cultural History: the Nagara-Kertagama by Rakawi Prapañca of Majapahit, 1365 A.D.*, 4 vols. (The Hague, 1960).

its existence in the form of a seventeenth-century manuscript. It is from these that the narrative of rulers and their achievements and, in general, the content as distinct from the shadowy outline of events is drawn. These sources would appear, therefore, to represent an account of Javanese history from the point of view of the periods in which they were written. But when one comes to consider their value as evidence for the events they describe several problems arise. In the first place it is obvious that, whatever may be their value as sources of their own times, such chronicles are not necessarily to be taken at their face value when they are reporting events of perhaps hundreds of years earlier. To what extent are they merely the repositories of oral tradition? How much of their content is legendary? One may easily strip away the obviously mythical elements of the story, but there can be no guarantee that the remaining narrative is an accurate one unless its broad outlines are supported by other evidence. And even where these sources are concerned with events nearer to themselves difficulties of a more subtle kind have been raised. It has been argued that these chronicles had a magical function to perform within their own society, to justify and to legitimize. They had to provide existing rulers with appropriate ancestries and to tell a story of the past which supported the authority of the present regime. They were thus forced to give an account of the events that ought to have occurred rather than of those that did in fact occur.

This sort of criticism has been raised, in particular, by the Dutch historian, C. C. Berg. Before him the historian, N. J. Krom, in his monumental *Hindu-Javanese History*, had been content, while examining literary sources critically, nonetheless to accept the possibility of a substratum of fact that textual examination could reveal. Berg's criticism of this approach was fundamental. The chronicles, in his view, could offer evidence for the kind of society which produced these works, for its values and its general structure; they could not provide evidence for events, though guesses might be made provided that one was aware of the real function, the magical function, of these chronicles.[22] In particular Berg brought his critical

[22] Berg's views are scattered through a series of articles in *Indonesië* and other journals. For a brief statement of them see C. C. Berg, "Javanese Historiography —A Synopsis of Its Evolution" and "The Work of Professor Krom," D. G. E. Hall (ed.), *Historians of South-East Asia* (London, 1961). See also J. G. de Casparis, "Historical Writing on Indonesia (Early Period)" in the same volume. For a criticism, see F. D. K. Bosch, "C. C. Berg: Ancient Javanese History," *Bijdragen tot de Taal-, Land- en Volkenkunde van Nederlandsch-Indië*, vol. 112, p. 1.

approach to bear on the general history of Madjapahit and cast doubt on whether this empire had really existed. The account of it given by Prapantja in the *Nagarakertagama* was held to be no more than a display of geographical knowledge! The areas over which suzerainty was claimed were known to Madjapahit but were certainly not controlled in any real sense by it.

Contemporary opinion appears to be swinging back from Berg's extreme position to a position a little nearer to the traditional one. The present tendency appears to be once again to accept the reality of Madjapahit as a considerable empire. And there is enough evidence to be found in Chinese chronicles, and in inscriptions, to confirm the broad outline of earlier fluctuations in dynastic fortunes. In any case for our purposes here the precise details are not the important thing. What is important is the general contribution of the Hindu-Javanese period to Indonesian culture and to her political organization. On the one hand the accommodating village was able to assimilate elements of Hinduism and Buddhism without great difficulty and on the other we have the sophistication of the distinct court culture, which remains an important ingredient in the Javanese view of the world. Among the distinguishing features of this culture were the importance of birth in determining rank, the existence of a series of levels and grades within the hereditary aristocracy, and the accompanying elaboration of a complex etiquette to guide the relations between inferior and superior. There were even different languages to be used according to whether a person was speaking "up" or "down." Etiquette placed an emphasis on polish and refinement of behavior; it prescribed an artificiality of politeness, so that the observance of the strict rules in social intercourse could become a kind of game, a complicated exercise in propriety and self-effacement. Politeness required the restraint and discipline of unruly feelings, and the preservation of a smooth and untroubled surface. The outward observances were linked with a mystical world-view in which, through contemplation, the apprehension of spiritual truths could make possible a discipline of one's external behavior—a bringing of it into line with the harmony of the universe. And the higher one's birth the more perfect was likely to be one's intuition of ultimate reality. The formalized code of aristocratic social behavior was at the same time a product of the monarchical system and a reinforcement of it.

Borrowed Forms and Local Genius

The precise extent to which this contribution represents an Indian penetration of an indigenous culture is a question to which we must now return more specifically. How far were the main forms of a traditional society preserved? And by what means were external influences conveyed to Indonesia?

The rise of Srivijaya in southern Sumatra and of Mataram and its successors in Java must be seen in the wider context of Asian commercial development, which by the middle of the first millennium of the Christian era had established a network of relations extending from China to the eastern Mediterranean, and of the accompanying spread of Indian influence in Southeast Asia as a whole. The origins of Southeast Asian trade are lost in the mists of time, but obviously there must have been a long history of commercial contacts between India and her neighbors extending far back beyond the emergence of what the French historian, Coedès, calls the "Hinduized states of South-East Asia." The first known of these states, that of Funan in Indo-China, makes its appearance in history in the first centuries A.D. Reference to it and to its neighbor, Champa, occur in Chinese chronicles.[23] Funan appears to have lasted until the sixth century when it was succeeded by the kingdom of Chenla and after the latter's collapse in the early eighth century, by a Khmer kingdom whose capital was established at Angkor at the end of the ninth century and whose magnificent profusion of temples, like that of Java, reflects a blending of Indian influence and local tradition.

At first glance it seems natural to interpret this extraordinary growth, over a wide area, of powerful states displaying roughly similar characteristics in terms of an Indian initiative imposed upon the more or less passive recipients. Such terms as Coedès' "Hinduized states" carry this suggestion of a predominantly one-way influence. So does the title of Quaritch Wales' book, *The Making of Greater India* (though its argument does not). And as Hall points out, the very terms "Indonesia" and "Indo-China" carry the same implication. It would now be generally agreed that the story was not simply one of the export of India's civilization to more benighted parts, though the degree to which this was so varied from area to area. In some places there was a more positive reception of external influence

[23] See Hall, *op. cit.*, Chap. II, for a summary of the evidence.

than in others. Earlier theories of the spread of Indian influence saw it as carried by waves of immigrants who established colonies overseas and thus became the foci for the diffusion of culture. It may seem not unreasonable to postulate such a development as a natural consequence of the development of trade. As commercial contacts expanded they might draw in their train more or less permanent settlers. However there is no evidence of such a process, and recent scholarship has tended to argue that it was not even a probable development given the character of the trade itself. It is here that van Leur's analysis becomes relevant once more. Van Leur argued that it was important in speaking of Asian trade to distinguish it from any form of Western capitalist commercial activity. He defined Western capitalism in terms of three main criteria—mass production based on a free labor market, a system of finance involving a stock market exchange system, and a free market for sales,[24] and he made a sharp distinction between this concept and the type of commercial activity to be found in the ancient Mediterranean world or in early Asian trade, in spite of their world-wide character. These trading systems were backed not by a system of free labor and mass production but by handicraft industry. Investment was not a systematic activity but an occasional one—an activity of rulers or of members of a patriciate who would invest from time to time, not as entrepreneurs or merchants, but simply as the financiers of a particular voyage. Finally, the actual trade was carried on by peddlers whose task was merely to collect and carry.[25] Thus, though royal treasuries, or the wealth of a ruling class, provided the finance for trade, the role of this aristocracy was a passive one. The handicraft traders and the peddlers were the active ones, travelling singly or in caravans, covering vast distances, and forming a foreign quarter in the cities of distant countries where they traded.

From this idealized model van Leur drew important conclusions about the diffusion of culture. Though the international trade was carried out on a world-wide basis, the fact that it was a peddling trade meant that it could not be the bearer of culture nor the vehicle of colonization. Indian peddlers, though they may have settled in Asian cities, remained separate from the surrounding society. They were in any case of lower social orders and were quite incapable of purveying the religious beliefs and ritual, the technical and artistic skills, or the sophisticated administrative procedures that were the main features

---

[24] Van Leur, "On Early Asian Trade," *loc. cit.*, p. 17.
[25] *Ibid.*, pp. 6ff.

ot the Indian contribution to Southeast Asian civilization.[26] It followed, in his view, that cultural influences could only have been the work of Brahmans, who were as far removed from trade as possible, and it must therefore have been the result of deliberate borrowing by the rulers of the recipient countries rather than the product of commercial influence or of any large degree of immigration. "The initiative for the coming of Indian civilization emanated from the Indonesian ruling groups, or was at least an affair of both the Indonesian dynasties and the Indian hierocracy." [27]

This hypothesis does provide a convincing rationale for the known facts. Trade might have played a greater part than van Leur suggests, and it should of course be noticed that trade itself was in any case not a one-way process. Indonesian traders were involved in the system and made their own contact with India as Indians did with Indonesia. But it seems probable that the development of the commercial contact at the peddling level should have been followed by the deliberate introduction of beliefs and rituals which fitted the existing Indonesian scene and could supply a consecration and legitimization of royal functions. This view postulates the emergence, at least on a small scale, of a degree of sophisticated political organization before the introduction of Hindu or Buddhist influence. The rulers of local principalities themselves must have been ready to adopt appropriate elements from Indian culture that could bolster their own authority.

The exact nature of the pre-Indian political units in Indonesia must remain a matter of speculation since exact evidence is not available. Clifford Geertz thinks that van Leur, in redressing earlier views of Indian migration, has leaned too far in the opposite direction and has overestimated the size and complexity of these states. In Geertz's view, indigenous development had probably been more limited—the growth of chieftains on a tribal basis bound by custom—and Hinduism therefore did in fact make all the difference to these rudimentary political units. It made "kings out of chiefs, towns out of villages, and temples out of spirit houses."[28] But this too is to speculate. What does seem clear is that Hinduism played a crucial part at least in consolidating the emergence of large political units,

[26] *Ibid.*, p. 99.
[27] *Ibid.*, p. 103. For a more recent development of the same thesis, see F. D. K. Bosch, "The Problem of the Hindu Colonisation of Indonesia" in his *Selected Studies in Indonesian Archaelogoy* (The Hague, 1961).
[28] Geertz, *The Development of the Javanese Economy*, (Massachusetts Institute of Technology, Center for International Studies, 1956), p. 80.

making available both organizational techniques and religious sanctions. The latter were particularly important.

Central to the Hindu-Javanese political system was the Brahmanic concept of the god-king, whose magical powers underlay the whole system of authority. The terrestrial order was regarded as a reflection of the cosmic order. The king in the terrestrial order was the counterpart of God and indeed was God. Below the ruler, though Indonesia did not assimilate the caste system of India, society was graded and rank was again supported by supernatural sanctions. Geertz puts the point well: "Spiritual excellence was correlated with political eminence and culminated in the immobile king, the incarnation of Vishnu or Shiva, meditating in his castle at the center of the universe. Spiritual power flowed outward and downward from its royal fountainhead, attenuating as it sank through each layer in the bureaucracy, draining weakly at last into the peasant masses."[29] In this way the growth of an aristocratic system, suited to the needs of an Indonesian agricultural economy, received its legitimation. Geertz goes on to develop in a brilliant paragraph an account of the appropriate values of the society in terms of the concepts *alus* and *kasar*:

> *Alus* means pure, refined, polished, polite, exquisite, ethereal, subtle, civilized, smooth. A man who speaks flawless high-Javanese is *alus*, as is the high-Javanese itself. A piece of cloth with intricate, subtle designs painted onto it is *alus*. An exquisitely played piece of music or a beautifully controlled dance step is *alus*. So is a smooth stone, a dog with his hair petted down, a far-fetched joke, or a clever poetic conceit. God is, of course, *alus* (as are all invisible spirits), and so is the mystical experience of Him. One's own soul and character are *alus* insofar as one emotionally comprehends the ultimate structure of existence; and one's behavior and actions are *alus* insofar as they are regulated by the delicate intricacies of the complex court-derived etiquette. *Kasar* is merely the opposite; impolite, rough, uncivilized; a badly played piece of music, a stupid joke, a cheap piece of cloth. Between these two poles the *prijaji* arranges everyone from peasant to king.[30]

This system of thought and belief was given a symbolic expression in city building. Just as the kingdom itself represented a microcosm of the universe so the royal capital in its turn was also, on a smaller though perhaps more perfect scale, a further microcosmic representation orientated to the four points of the compass, and

[29] *The Religion of Java*, p. 232.
[30] *Ibid.*

centered on the palace of the ruler.[31] To borrow the phrase applied by Redfield to Maya civilization, it was a "quadrilateral, layered universe" which was symbolized in this way.[32] Again in temple architecture the same world view is reflected. Javanese temples combined more than one function. They were temples—places of Hindu or Buddhist worship. They were also *tjandis*—monumental tombs.[33] They thus represented a fusion of indigenous practices of ancestor worship with religious beliefs imported from India. This is precisely the sort of fusion at which the Javanese have shown themselves particularly adept, and the tendency to equate kings and gods was part of this blending of traditions. Statues of the former were used as representations of the latter,[34] so that divinity and kingship became blurred—a successful attempt, says Wagner, "to attain a synthesis of ancestor cult and Hinduism: the prince becomes an incarnation of the divinity."[35] And the *tjandi* as a whole is, by the same token, at once Mt. Meru, the mountain of God, and a representation in stone of the nature of the universe itself.[36]

The Buddhist stupa, Borobodur, may illustrate some of these characteristics. It is not like many other monuments, a tomb, nor is it a temple with an interior: rather it is a stupa built around the summit of a hill and rising in nine receding layers to the crowning pinnacle. Its great size may be gauged from the fact that the galleries around the terraces are together over three miles in length. From the two terraces at the base of the monument there rise four layers which are composed of galleries containing some thousands of sculptured reliefs which present incidents in the life of the Buddha and illustrate Buddhist texts.[37] Above these rise three circular tiers on which stand

---

[31] Robert Heine-Geldern, "Conceptions of State and Kingship in South East Asia," *Far Eastern Quarterly*, Vol. II, No. 1 (November 1942).

[32] Redfield, *op. cit.*, p. 64.

[33] The term *tjandi* is used in Indonesia as a generic term for ancient monuments, though strictly it should refer only to those which are sepulchres. But in fact a great number of Indonesian *tjandis* are tombs.

[34] For example the statue of Airlangga in his mausoleum presented him as Vishnu. Heine-Geldern, *loc. cit.*

[35] Wagner, *op. cit.*, p. 104.

[36] See, *e.g.*, H. G. Quaritch Wales, *The Mountain of God* (London, 1953).

[37] At the very base a further set of reliefs has been covered over, for reasons which are not clear, by the stone work of the bottom layer of the monument. See Hall, *op. cit.*, pp. 49-50, for an account of the explanation given by J. G. de Casparis (*Prasasti Indonesia*, Vol. I) which involves interpreting the Borobodur simultaneously from the point of view of Buddhism and from that of ancestor worship.

small stupas, each containing under its bell-like shape a statue of the Buddha. The monument as a whole has been taken to represent a "textbook of Buddhism,"[38] and a symbol of the individual's stages toward perfection.

Because of its size, the fact that it is not a burial place, and the fact that it is Buddhist rather than Hindu, the Borobodur is perhaps a special case, but it demonstrates on the grand scale some of the features of later *tjandis*—and in particular the pyramidal shape representing the cosmic mountain, and indeed standing as a model of the cosmos itself. Similarly the kingdom, with its hierarchical aristocratic order, was modelled on the same symbolic lines.

In making the point that Hinduism provided a powerful ideological contribution to the creation of new political forms, it is not really necessary to consider whether Hinduism made it possible for monarchy to develop or whether it was accepted as a useful ideological prop to support existing monarchies. Such a chicken-and-egg question would be worthwhile if the evidence were available to answer it. As it is not, one can merely point to the appropriateness of Indian cosmological views for the society in which they flourished in Indonesia. Perhaps it would be sufficient to see Hinduism as offering both a projection and a legitimation of monarchical order.[39]

If one accepts the view that the ritualistic elements of Hinduism were deliberately borrowed, it would be natural to expect that the borrowing would be limited and selective, adapted to the needs of existing Indonesian society. Certainly in the field of artistic expression it is clear that Indian motifs were handled in a distinctively Indonesian way, though the degree to which Indian styles appeared to dominate the inspiration of local craftsmen varied from place to place and time to time. In examining this question Quaritch Wales distinguishes between cases of extreme acculturation, where traditional inspiration was more or less completely submerged, and cases where a less extreme impact was made. In distinguishing between the two types of situation he uses the concept of "local genius" which might be destroyed under extreme contact, but which in less extreme cases remains visible, revealing itself as a preference for the more congenial elements of the borrowed culture, which it was able to adapt to its own purposes.[40] Local genius in the latter situation is

---

[38] Hall, *op. cit.*, p. 43.

[39] Geertz, *Development of the Javanese Economy*, p. 80.

[40] H. G. Quaritch Wales, *The Making of Greater India* (2nd ed., London, 1961), pp. 17-18.

not merely one element in a mixture. "In conditioning the recipients to foreign stimulus," said Wales, "it provides the active agency which moulds the borrowed material, giving it an original twist and at the same time preserving and emphasizing the distinctive character of the evolution." In Java, the local genius was able to retain its controlling and directing role. Early architectural examples show a dominant Indian influence which, in later examples, is modelled in a distinctive way by local craftsmen until, with the architectural remains of Madjapahit, there is apparent a resurgence of pre-Hindu culture imposing itself on borrowed forms.[41] In practical terms the distinction is based on a consideration of over-all architectural design, of the motifs used and of the method of carving.

The Village and the Court

It is implied in what has been said that Hinduism, developed under Brahman influence in Indonesia, was essentially a court culture, providing beliefs, rituals, and accompanying artistic forms appropriate to the needs of a ruling class, and that therefore its impact on the village might well be an extremely limited one. In Bali Hinduism became and remained a living religion, but elsewhere the metaphor of a "thin and flaking glaze" may be more appropriate to describe the influence of Indian culture on the village. It was much more of a veneer perhaps than was later to be the case with Islam. As the center of agrarian life in an intensive agricultural economy, the Javanese village, though it has its distinctive forms of organization which mark it off from villages in southern or western Sumatra, in Kalimantan or in Sulawesi, nonetheless has strong links with types of village organization elsewhere, not merely in Indonesia but in Southeast Asia as a whole. And it may be argued that the basic and more or less common features are more important, after all, than the differences from region to region. In this way one is tempted to see a village tradition and a village type of organization as an ideal type—a society with an enormous capacity for absorbing specific cultural influences from outside without changing its essential character. Such models, of course, have only a limited usefulness and their correspondence with reality is never entirely complete; but the Javanese village does appear to have preserved, to a considerable extent, its traditional characteristics—its belief in an all-pervading spirit world, its sense of solidarity and harmony, its conservatism—while

[41] *Ibid.*, pp. 123-4.

changes were going on above the village level and while village units were being drawn into the broader political unit of the principality.

Village and court together nonetheless formed complementary parts of one society. Indian cultural influence stimulated this process and was, in effect, imported into a situation that was ready to receive it. The creation of an intensive agriculture based upon an irrigation system was certainly an achievement of the Javanese before the impact of India, and this achievement imposed its own logic upon political developments. A stable agricultural society provided the opportunity for the growth of civilization and indeed demanded an adequate political and administrative system that could provide the necessary services to agriculture. Tribute levied in support of a court, with all of the appurtenances of court life, represented one side of a coin whose other side was the fact that intensive agriculture required the supervision of a political unit extending beyond the individual village. If the *Kraton* of the prince depended upon its ability to draw tribute from the village by force or persuasion (hence its readiness to use whatever supernatural sanctions were available to confirm and justify its authority), the village in its turn depended upon princely power for its security and for its good governance in relation to its neighbors. At the same time the village, while enfolded within the broader political unit, retained a good deal of its own independence. It was the source of labor and the center of agricultural production. It had its own customary forms of government. It was not entirely without its own bargaining power against the ruler, especially in the areas remote from the court center. It was in a sense a small, self-contained republic.

It was this complementary relationship between the peasant and his ruler which must be regarded as of permanent importance when one attempts to assess the contribution to Indonesian society of the Hindu-Javanese period. The formation of kingdoms represented an adjustment between the traditions of the village and the demands of the monarchy, and the former retained their vitality while being drawn into the greater unity. However introduced, the principles by which the greater unity was established represented a contribution that Indian civilization could make to Indonesia. The principles of hierarchy, and of monarchy at the apex, were principles which were necessary to the development of Indonesian culture and it seems natural that Indian influence was able to reinforce indigenous tendencies and should have helped to determine the precise form they took. In this context the question of the precise degree of cultural borrowing, though important for its own sake, becomes irrelevant for our general theme.

There must be mentioned a further consequence of the Hindu-Javanese period: It consolidated and confirmed the dominant role of Java in the history of the archipelago. After about the eleventh century with the decline of Srivijaya, the island of Java acquired an importance it was never to lose. Its supremacy was not to be unchallenged. The Malacca sultanate, for example, was to play in the fifteenth century a part not unlike that played earlier by Srivijaya and was to rival Javanese hegemony. But even during this period the history of the region was one of interaction between Javanese power and Malacca's commercial empire, not of a Javanese eclipse. It may be doubted whether one can write of Indonesia as a continuing entity before the nineteenth century, but insofar as it is legitimate to do so, its history is very much one of fluctuating rivalries in which the island of Java is always a central factor, balancing the power of rival states. This pattern was to be observed clearly at the close of the Hindu-Javanese period.

Madjapahit, the last of the Hindu-Javanese empires, fell, probably, in the early sixteenth century, but before this its power had been threatened by the gradual penetration into the archipelago of a new external force—that of Islam. The Malacca sultanate established in the early fifteenth century became a center for the spread of Islam through the islands, but the development was not merely a matter of religious conversion: political and commercial motives were intertwined with those of conviction and, at least to some extent, Islam was a weapon that could be used to challenge the dominance of Madjapahit.

The challenge went beyond political expediency, however, and in turning to examine the penetration of Islam, we are again faced by the general question of Indonesia's ability to absorb cultural influences from outside while still preserving her own identity.

THREE

THE INFLUENCE OF ISLAM

The eastern Javenese kingdom of Madjapahit represented the climax of Hindu-Javanese civilization. It ended for the time the dynastic struggles which had marked the growth of the monarchical order in Java, and, even if its own territorial claims were exaggerated, it did establish a considerable empire extending beyond Java and powerful enough to weld diverse regions into a unity more complete than had so far been seen in the archipelago. Even the mighty Srivijaya had not enjoyed such unchallenged authority. Madjapahit, however, was Hindu-Javanese with a difference. Its imperial sway was not based merely on the traditional sinews of power—the control of agricultural wealth. It had established itself also as a commercial empire, controlling trade routes and centering entrepot activities in the ports of Java's north coast. In effect, it combined, in terms of political order, the characteristics of Srivijaya and the old Mataram.

Such a combination of land-based power and maritime power was a natural development, for the growth of the series of kingdoms in central and eastern Java between the eighth and thirteenth centuries had almost certainly taken place against the background of a gradual expansion of international trade. Brief reference has already been made to the evolution of commercial relations linking the Far East, Southeast Asia, India, and western Asia in what was really a single system with its westward extension penetrating into the Mediterranean. Persians, Arabs, Indians, Chinese, all participated in the collection and carrying of goods, and such ports as Cambai, the port of Gujerat in northwestern India, and Calicut on the Malabar Coast of India became major international emporia. The trade comprised many items—raw silk, textiles, gold, sandalwood, porcelain, a variety of handicraft goods—Indonesia's own contribution consisting chiefly of the supply of fragrant woods, especially camphor and benzoin, and pepper, nutmeg, and mace.[1] This commercial development served as the natural basis for the strength of Srivijaya, which was strategically placed on the direct route from India to the Far East, but it did not entirely pass by the land-based kingdoms of Java. Eastern Java, in particular, had its own strategic advantages in relation to the collection of spices from the eastern islands of the archipelago. First Kadiri, one of the successor kingdoms that followed Airlangga, and then Singhosari, had played its part in this commerce and had established itself as a power able ultimately to challenge Srivijaya. The conflict between the two thus foreshadowed the emergence of Madjapahit, whose more dramatic expansion was to follow in the thirteenth century and was to lead to two centuries of empire over both rice fields and trade routes.

But Madjapahit's commercial predominance was not to remain unchallenged, for the development of a new commercial power at Malacca in the early fifteenth century represented competition of no mean order. Originally a small fishing village, Malacca developed rapidly as a center of trade under Paramesvara, a refugee prince from Palembang, who had been driven from his territory by Madjapahit. His conversion to Islam made his new realm a center of Moslem traders and aided its development as an entrepot port in the Strait of Malacca. In theory Madjapahit claimed suzerainty over the Malay Peninsula (as did also Siam) and therefore over the new sultanate. In fact, however, the rapid growth of Malacca placed it in a position where it could ignore these rival claims and establish itself effectively as an independent commercial realm. By virtue of its excellent position, it was thus able, as Hall puts it [2] to "thrust itself into the trade route in spices . . . from the Moluccas to India." In so doing, of course, it cut one of the sinews of the strength of Madjapahit itself. The north coast ports of Java, through which the spice trade had been handled, were gradually drawn into the orbit of the new commercial power and in time developed the desire to detach themselves from Madjapahit as their new trade links consolidated themselves.

But the story was not simply one of changing patterns of trade.

[1] Van Leur, op. cit., p. 121-124.
[2] Hall, op. cit., p. 180.

A crucial element in the decline of Madjapahit was the fact that Malacca was a center for the spread of Islam throughout the archipelago as well as for the forging of new commercial ties. Indeed the two processes were inseparable. The Islamic faith had begun to filter into the Indies before the rise of Malacca, of course. Arab traders had played their part in the operation of the Asian trade routes even before Mohammed and the advent of Islam,[3] and after that watershed, Arab peddlers became bearers of the faith as well as merchants. The spread of Islam was aided by the conversion of Gujerat, whose merchants were active in the Strait and the archipelago. Marco Polo on his return journey to Europe in 1292 reported a Moslem community in northern Sumatra, and it was from such footholds that the gradual diffusion of Islam was made possible. Conversion of coastal rulers rather than of populations in general was the main method by which Moslem observance was extended.

The process was slow until the rise of Malacca provided a central power house for the rapid proselytization of the Peninsula and the islands. In Java, in particular, the maritime principalities of the north coast, Demak, Djepara, Tuban, Madura, Surabaja, as they were drawn into the commercial orbit of Malacca found themselves drawn simultaneously into her spiritual orbit. From these ports the faith was carried, again by commerce, to the Moluccas and Celebes. But though commerce was the vehicle, the process of conversion no doubt reflected a variety of motives. Religious conviction and commercial advantage both played their parts and so, it is clear, did political advantage. When the harbor principalities, caught up in the activities of a new commercial power, sought to establish their independence from Madjapahit, Islam served as a useful ideological weapon in their struggle, as it was later to be for Indonesians in general against the European. Islam's contribution to this struggle was twofold. It offered certainly a symbol of resistance, but more fundamentally it constituted an alternative to the whole Hindu view of the world. In bringing man face to face with God without the necessity of a mediating priesthood or a complicated ritual, it implied a doctrine of equality which could offer a powerful solvent for the hierarchical order of Madjapahit. It thus had an appeal to the harbor states and as the fifteenth century proceeded there occurred the gradual detachment of Madjapahit's periphery—a development which, in its broad outlines, fits into the pattern to which we have

[3] *Ibid.*, p. 176.

already referred of interaction between the military power of a land-based empire and the commercial might of maritime states.

The exact date of Madjapahit's fall is obscure. It had been subjected to attack by Demak in 1478 and, it would seem, to subsequent onslaughts from a coalition of the Islamized coastal principalities,[4] but the Portuguese, after their conquest of Malacca in 1511, found in eastern Java that a Hindu kingdom shorn of its grandeur was still resisting the Islamic coast. Its final collapse was followed by a shift of power from eastern to central Java and, during the sixteenth century, the rise of a new inland state whose name, Mataram, carried echoes of the earlier state of King Sanjaya and of the later tenth-century Mataram. But the new Mataram was not to represent a resurgence of Hindu civilization. Like Madjapahit, it also had to contend with the power of the coastal states, and its rulers, in their ultimately successful struggle with those states, found it convenient themselves to embrace Islam.

Mataram's conflict with its coastal rivals took place in a rapidly changing environment. By their conquest of Malacca in 1511, the Portuguese had established themselves as heirs to the Sultanate's commercial predominance. Control of the Strait, where ships from the Far East and from the Spice Islands converged, was sufficient to confer this upon the Portuguese as it had formerly upon the Malacca sultanate and before that upon Srivijaya, but the religious tie, so important in the preceding century, was now broken. The challenge of the Portuguese was a factor in encouraging the subsequent consolidation of Islam throughout the archipelago; at the same time it had repercussions for Demak and its allies in their war with Mataram. At the end of the sixteenth century, the Moslem Mataram under Senopati defeated its Moslem rivals and re-established in central and eastern Java the dominance of an agricultural kingdom. Bantam, also a Moslem state, controlled the west of Java, and it was these two powers that were to face the Dutch in the seventeenth century.

The Coming of Islam—Adaptation

This story of the gradual Islamization of Indonesia raises a number of questions of importance for an understanding of Islam's later role in the archipelago. Indonesia today has rejected for herself the idea of an Islamic state, but in many respects she appears nonetheless to be an Islamic country. The central position of mosque and prayer

[4] Hall, *op. cit.*, p. 184.

houses in thousands of villages, the observance of the simple rituals of the faith—the repetition of the confession and the call to prayer five times a day—the importance placed upon the making of the pilgrimage to Mecca, the respect paid to teachers learned in the law, would all seem to bear witness to the completeness of her conversion at least in terms of the outward forms. In particular the widespread observance of the fasting month of Ramadan would seem to the ordinary observer to point to a real and not merely a nominal adherence to the faith. How far are these appearances deceptive? The nature of Islam would seem to preclude half-hearted compromise. It is an austere religion. Lacking a complex ecclesiastical organization, its appeal is to the devotion of the individual. The sense of community is important, certainly, but the community (*ummat*) is made up of those who are faithful, that is to say of individual believers. And their devotion in theory must be complete. The very word Islam means submission, complete and unconditional, excluding, so it would seem, any mere nominal adherence or any tolerance of competing views of the world. By its nature it was hardly a faith which would be expected to blend easily into the syncretic Indonesian environment.

In fact, however, a good deal of blending did take place, though it was not a regular or even process. The reality of Indonesia's acceptance of Islam has clearly been a matter of degree varying widely both from person to person and from area to area. There are those who accept the absolute requirements of the faith and who would, if they could, make over society to fit the most extreme Islamic image; and there are others who, while calling themselves Moslems, have no such single-minded devotion. In Java, particularly, Moslem observance and belief often sit lightly on believers so that the genuinely devout Moslem, the *santri*, stands clearly apart from the man whose religious belief is compounded of elements of animism and magic and mysticism as well as the teaching of the Prophet, and whose behavior is guided by the custom of the village rather than by the precise, rigid prescriptions of Islamic law. In some other areas conversion was more complete. With some exceptions the main centers of the faith in Indonesia have lain outside the area of the ethnic Javanese—in west Java, west Sumatra and Atjeh, in south Sulawesi—and in these areas it represents a major ingredient in local cultures.

In considering this problem of the reality of Indonesia's adherence to Islam a number of questions need to be distinguished. Was the new faith more acceptable to some elements in the Indonesian community than to others? How far was its uneven success due to differences of emphasis which may be discerned within Islam itself? Despite its ideals of single-minded devotion, did Islam, in seeking its converts, show itself willing to compromise with custom?

There are good reasons for giving an affirmative answer to the first of these questions: Indonesian Islam appears to have been more acceptable in the commercial centers of the region and less at home within the framework of an inland agricultural society. In its origins, as we have seen, the spread of the faith was closely associated with the pattern of international trade that enfolded the Peninsula and the islands, and it was no accident that it established its strongest footholds in the coastal ports—in north Sumatra, in the great Malacca emporium, in Demak, Djepara, Tuban, and Makassar. There were several features of the faith that helped to explain this pattern of diffusion. Attention has already been drawn in particular to the Islamic acceptance of the principle of the equality of believers, who, collectively, made up the Islamic community—a principle more suited to the world of trade than was the principle of hierarchy on which the Hinduistic state was built. Beyond that the very simplicity, and indeed the austerity, of the Islamic faith might be regarded as appropriate to the needs of a trading class. So might the individualism implicit in the absence of a priesthood. In the cosmopolitan ports of the Indies, where people from many different parts of the world clustered in their separate quarters, preserved their separate identities, and met on a common footing only in the market place, a faith which made no distinction of race or class could cut across communal divisions and help to establish a new social unity. In the light of these features, the connection between Islam and commerce seems a natural one, and it has led one observer to ascribe to Islam in Indonesia a role not unlike that ascribed by Weber to Protestantism in Europe—the role of handmaiden to a commercial class. "For Hinduism's attempt to sacralize a political community built around inequalities in military power, Islam substituted an attempt to sacralize a commercial community, built around commonalities in economic motivation." [5] Such a thesis helps to explain the fact that the

[5] Clifford Geertz, *The Development of the Javanese Economy*, p. 91.

original strongholds of the faith—the areas where indigenous traders have continued to play a leading role—have remained among the most devoutly Moslem areas of Indonesia today.

The conversion of Mataram may seem to offer an exception to this general thesis. Here the social organization of an inland agricultural state did not seem to present a bar to the acceptance of the new teaching. In fact, however, the conversion of Mataram was a different sort of process from that of the north coast states of Java. Mataram adopted Islam in part as a means of self-defense against the coastal states. It was a matter of political expediency and the conversion itself, if the religious texture of modern Java is an indication, was a more superficial conversion than that which had taken place on the coast. Insofar as Islam was able to penetrate below the surface of inland Javanese society, it did so by adapting itself in considerable measure to existing patterns of belief and custom.

That it was able to accommodate itself in this way is significant for the second and third of the questions we have asked, for it suggests that Indonesian Islam in practice was less uncompromising than would be expected in theory. The great Dutch Islamicist, Snouck Hurgronje, remarked that "In the course of its victorious progress through the world, the Mohammedan religion has been compelled to adopt a vast quantity of new matter which was originally quite alien to it, but which appeared indispensable to the majority of its adherents, and all of which has now been exalted to be law and doctrine." [6] In Indonesia's case the ability to make this sort of compromise appears in fact to have been partly due to the particular variant of Islam which was offering itself.

A vital division to be observed in the history of Islam has been that between the legalism of the schools on the one hand and the search for a more vital form of life and practice on the other, between a dry concern for orthodoxy and a tolerance for the idea of direct and perhaps mystical religious experience as a way of truth. The desire for a more personal and emotional form of belief was associated in particular with the Sufi orders which, from the thirteenth to the eighteenth centuries formed the chief proselytizing elements in Islam. It is perhaps a natural development in the growth of any system of formal religion that an initial prophetic stage is likely to be followed by a solidification or ossification of what began as an appeal to the

[6] Christiaan Snouck Hurgronje, *The Achehnese*, Trans. A. W. S. O'Sullivan (Leyden, 1960), II, 313.

heart. As a result there develops a need for renewal from time to time, and a continuing tension is likely to emerge between the Church and the Saints, between orthodoxy and incipient heresy, between outer forms and inner light. In Islam the accretion of the Tradition upon the Koran and the development of a scholastic approach, created its own vested interests engaged in an analysis of the Law and the Tradition, and this solidification in turn provoked its own solution. Sufism could offer satisfaction to the religious instincts of the general body of followers by its more directly personal and emotional approach.[7] And Sufism as the missionary arm of Islam was willing to allow a degree of accommodation between Islamic orthodoxy and the other religious traditions from which it sought converts. The precise role of Sufi missionaries in the conversion of Indonesia is a matter of speculation, but there are good reasons for accepting the view of A. H. Johns that they probably played a dominant part.[8] He sees them as accompanying traders, associating themselves with craft guilds, and making a significant appeal through their ability to adjust themselves to local beliefs and through the fact that their mystical version of Islam had, in any case, more of an appeal than other versions in a country where animism and Hindu mysticism had already made a compromise with each other. In Java the Sufis "face the Shiva-Buddha mystics on equal terms as mystics to mystic, to teach the supremacy of the new religion."[9] Beyond the harbor states they were of use to rulers, giving royal authority a new legitimacy and turning rajahs into sultans. They were able also to accommodate themselves without too much difficulty to the existing social environment below the court.

So while the needs and values of commerce were important in aiding Indonesia's conversion, equally important was the particular variant of Islam that was being offered. Islam came to Indonesia by way of India—as Benda puts it, it was "filtered through the religious experience of India,"[10]—and had thus acquired mystical elements that fitted it to operate within the Indonesian setting. The process of adaptation was a two-way process. In much the same way as Hindu art had been subjected to a process of selection of some

[7] H. A. R. Gibb, *Mohammedanism: An Historical Survey* (London, O. U. P., 1961), p. 135.

[8] A. H. Johns, "Sufism as a Category in Indonesian Literature and History," *Journal of Southeast Asian History*, Vol. II, No. 2 (July 1961), p. 13.

[9] John's, *loc. cit.*, p. 17.

[10] Harry J. Benda, *The Crescent and the Rising Sun* (The Hague, 1958), p. 12.

features, rejection of others, and to a gradual modification of its character, so Islamic teaching, in seeking to change existing belief and practice, found itself able—and was indeed compelled—in some measure to base itself upon those existing forms.

This capacity was of special importance at the village level where the evidence of syncretic adaptation is particularly obvious. The Indonesian peasant finds no great difficulty in combining in varying mixtures his obligations as a Moslem with his acceptance of older beliefs and customs. The propitiation of spirits, the observance of customary rituals surrounding the main stages of life, the resort to magical practices in curing illness may all be accepted by the same person who is ready to observe Moslem law in marriage, to accept the Moslem ritual of circumcision, or to follow the daily pattern of prayer, the weekly community worship, and the annual month of fasting. This represents in parts of Indonesia a genuine blending.

At the same time, while Indonesia's syncretism is a byword, it must not be overly stressed. There was certainly a mutual tolerance between competing traditions, different beliefs, different world views. There was also tension. Custom could absorb Islam and Islam could go far toward adapting itself to custom, but there remained, none-theless, an opposition between the two, just as there was a measure of adjustment between them.

This was partly a simple matter of opposition between the more faithful and the less faithful. Any religion is likely to display such a division and must come to terms with the indifference of a large part of its followers, contenting itself with a mere nominal acceptance of the outward forms of the faith. But this was not the whole story in Indonesia. The pull of custom was not merely the inertia of indifference in the face of the demands of an austere religion. It was a positive pull. In the more fervently Moslem areas of Sumatra, in Atjeh or in Minangkabau, where Islam penetrated much more deeply into the social fabric than it did in Java, a distinct tension has existed between those who might be described as customary leaders of society and the religious leaders of society. The election of village heads in Minangkabau is a case in point. Village headmen are usually drawn from clan leaders whose standing is determined by that society's matrilineal kinship system. In these circumstances the con-nection between clan leadership and the village headship represents the pull of *adat* or customary law against which religious leadership is set. Status as conferred by customary authority does not coincide with the status accompanying religious authority. The tension here is not between the devout and the indifferent; it is a tension which is clearly related to status and which illustrates the problems that arise when different but overlapping status systems exist within one society. In Java the division between *santri* and *abangan* also constitutes, at least to some extent, a tension between religion and *adat*, though the status element in the conflict is not so clearly marked in this case. *Abangan* beliefs and attitudes reflect an adherence to a more ancient village tradition than that of Islam. There are areas where the Islamic strand in the village tradition is clearly dominant and where the influence of the religious teacher, the *kiyayi* and the *ulama* may be paramount in determining village leadership. There are others where *abangan* views are dominant. But in either case the division between the two is accompanied often by strong feeling.[11]

Recognition of tensions such as these is vital for an understanding of Islam's role in Indonesia's history. The claims of the new religion as it began to spread through the islands were in theory absolute. In practice it was prepared to settle for less, and it became, therefore, as Geertz terms it, a "variant"—an additional strand in a complex of traditions. There were many who did accept its absolute claims. There were others who did not. That it could be no more than a variant helps to throw into relief the peculiar and diverse character of Indonesia's society itself. We have noticed already the continuing autonomy of the village and the village tradition even as these were brought within the overarching framework of the Hindu kingdom. The aristocratic authority of the kingdom was, in a sense, balanced by the independent authority of the village and even the ideological weapons provided by Hinduism were not able to forge an indivisible political or social unity. The same fate awaited Islam. It could not provide a rationale that could bring village and court and also market into one political and social order.

The Indonesian tradition, then, remained compounded of many elements, some of which stand out more clearly than others. It is useful to distinguish three religious outlooks characteristic of three social

[11] For an account of the persistence of a cleavage between orthodox and syncretist elements in Javanese society, see Robert R. Jay, *Religion and Politics in Rural Central Java* (Cultural Report Series No. 12, Southeast Asia Studies, New Haven: Yale University, 1963).

groups—the spirit worship and custom orientation of the village, which vary in detail from area to area; the refinement, sensibility, and civilization of aristocratic classes; and the purer Islamic outlook that has been associated with the trading community. This classification is useful but not exhaustive, however. It is essentially a Javanese model and needs the additional recognition of other ethnic and minority variants. Nor is it even a very precise model within itself for the reason that the Islamic variant overlaps the other two. The *abangan* tradition of the village community, as we have seen, is a compound of Islamic as well as earlier traditions. The Islam of the *santri* is not itself confined to the market place. There are devout as well as merely nominal Moslems in the ranks of the *priyayi*. Moreover the classification gives rise to the danger of confusing distinct categories. The category *santri* is really a category of a different kind from *abangan* and *priyayi* in that it relates only to belief and not, as they do, to a mixture of belief and status.[12] Nonetheless the distinction between the three variants is sufficiently clear to make the classification a useful one, and it does draw attention to competing views of the world that are not easily to be reconciled with each other.

Islam as a Symbol of Anticolonialism

These divisions were to be politically important during the colonial period. As Dutch rule consolidated itself in Java and began to penetrate more deeply into the outer islands, Islam came to offer a symbol of common resistance to alien domination. That it could do so was in part the result of the increasing depth of Islamic religious influence, for the process of Indonesia's conversion was a gradual and continuing one. The textbook picture of the diffusion of Islam in the fifteenth century is misleading in its suggestion of rapidity and completeness. Certainly, as we have indicated, the conversion of Mataram was not a conversion in any genuinely religious sense; it merely provided the opportunity for a work of proselytization, which was to be spread over the succeeding centuries. The nineteenth century saw a revival of Moslem orthodoxy or at least of a more rigorous adherence to the basic elements of the faith—a development that drew some of

---

[12] But notice Benda's argument—that the Moslem leader who associated himself with the functions of secular rule, the *penghulu*, became in effect "part and parcel of *priyayi* civilization," while the independent *ulama* became the nucleus of *santri* civilization (*The Crescent and the Rising Sun*, p. 15).

its inspiration from external sources. In the late-eighteenth century the Wahhabi movement in Arabia had attacked the laxity which was considered to be corrupting the faith. Wahhabism represented a puritan challenge that appealed for a return to the original sternness and simplicity of Islam, and it foreshadowed later, more sophisticated movements of Islamic reform. This development had an important impact in Indonesia as greater numbers of people undertook the pilgrimage and thus came into direct contact with the Arabic homeland of their religion.[13] The emphasis upon a purer and more rigorous belief, which they brought back with them, was accompanied by a successful attempt on the part of Islam to strike deeper roots within rural as well as urban society. This process had political side effects. It created, in fact, a religious base of opposition to Dutch authority—a potential rallying point for discontent. In some cases resistance was open—or at least movements of open resistance took on an Islamic character—as in Diponegoro's challenge to Dutch rule in Java in 1825 or the long-drawn-out Padri War in west Sumatra in the 1820s and 1830s. At the end of the century, the Atjeh War forced the Dutch to make their greatest single military effort in bringing the Indies under control and in return evoked an appeal to the idea of a holy war to expel the infidel. In the twentieth century Islam formed the basis of the first mass organization of the modern nationalist movement, Sarekat Islam.

Faced by the political implications of Islam the Dutch, for their part, tended to base their own authority upon customary leaders who, while they were at least nominally Moslem, were in status competition with Moslem religious leaders—upon the *priyayi* in Java and upon small princes or upon *adat* chiefs outside Java.[14] Such a policy tended to accentuate existing tensions between religion and custom, and it helped to discredit in the eyes of their fellows those who were willing to be drawn into the colonial administrative machine. The practice of using Indonesia's rulers as administrators was thus instrumental in eroding traditional patterns of authority and in strengthening the hand of *ulama* in rural society.[15] This is not to say that Islam was the chief basis of nationalism. It will be seen that a secular na-

---

[13] Benda, *op. cit.*, p. 17. For a study of some of the political, social and economic significances of the pilgrimage, see Jacob Vredenbregt, "The Haddj," *Bijdragen tot de Taal-, Land- en Volkenkunde*, Vol. 118 (1962).

[14] Benda, *op. cit.*, pp. 13-20.

[15] *Ibid.*, p. 16.

tionalist movement came to form the core of resistance to the Dutch in the 1920s and 1930s. But the Islamic element in nationalism continued to be important.

Moslem Reformers, Moslem Conservatives

To the tension between *santri* and *abangan* or, more generally, between Islam and *adat*, must be added differences and divisions within the Moslem community itself. The renewal of "orthodox" currents of thought in the nineteenth century had involved a degree of struggle against the mystical characteristics which had marked the early growth of Indonesia's Islam. In the twentieth century this struggle came to mingle with a contest between modern and more conservative currents of thought.

The Reformist movement which had its origins in Cairo at the end of the nineteenth century was concerned, in part, with the purification of the faith by the removal of the scholastic accretions which had obscured the teachings of the Prophet. It aimed also at the maintenance of the revived orthodoxy against such subtle compromises with pre-Islamic beliefs and practices as had been part and parcel of Islam's expansion in Indonesia. But it set its sights well beyond these goals and sought an accommodation between Islamic teaching and the modern world. The Reformers believed that a purified doctrine—a doctrine based on reason—could be reconciled with the needs of science and contemporary thought and that it could enable Islam to meet the challenges of social change. In particular such a forward looking faith could be expected to strike roots within those emergent middle classes whose members were not to be satisfied by the narrow faith of the rural *ulama*.

In Indonesia the new development found its expression in the formation, in 1912, of the reformist society Muhammadiyah which, through its own schools, and its cluster of subsidiary organizations, embarked upon a major educational task of reforming Islamic thought and doctrine. Unlike the mass nationalist organization, Sarekat Islam, formed in the same year, Muhammadiyah did not pursue a course of political action. Its approach to the problem of reforming Islamic teaching, however, did ultimately have political implications: in due course it contributed to the growth of intellectual Moslem opposition to the colonial regime. In the long term the division which it created between itself and the force of conservative Islam was eventually to carry over into divisions between Moslem political parties in independent Indonesia.[16]

Political consequences apart, the contrast between these differing currents of thought can be observed in the context of a variety of doctrines and practical issues. Geertz in his *Religion of Java*[17] lists five questions in particular on which progressive thought found itself in some degree at variance with conservatism. The conservative tends to take a fatalistic view of man's relations with God whereas the modernist emphasizes the virtue of human effort. The conservative tends to deny a distinction between secular and religious life and insists that religion penetrates all departments of life, whereas the modernist tends to operate as though there were a degree of independence between the two (though he does continue to affirm that religion underlies all departments of human activity at least in a broad sense). The conservative tends to be readier to accept an accommodation with non-Islamic beliefs and ritual while the modernist insists upon the purification of the faith. The conservative tends to emphasize the reality of religious experience while the modernist tends to stress outward behavior. Finally, the conservative tends to be more scholastic in his approach to the faith while the modernist stresses reason and uses practical arguments to justify particular actions.

These are test issues which offer a rough means of classification. It would be misleading, in applying the tests, to speak of them as tests of orthodoxy. Though the term reformist is applied to the movement of which Muhammadiyah was a part, and though this movement was concerned in its own eyes with a task of purification, it begs the question to see it as an orthodox movement. Indeed the term orthodox is sometimes applied to the conservative Moslem rather than to the reformist Moslem precisely because the latter did appear more willing to compromise with the experience of the modern world. In fact both sides could claim to be orthodox and the question of what constituted orthodoxy was the very question at stake.

Like so many of the antitheses with which we have been dealing, this modernist–conservative distinction can only be made in very broad terms. It did not coincide clearly with socio-economic patterns

[16] For the links between *Muhammadiyah* and the Masjumi party in rivalry with NU in Java and *Perti* in Sumatra, see H. Feith, in *The Indonesian Elections of 1955* (Ithaca, 1957), pp. 33-35.

[17] Geertz, *The Religion of Java*, pp. 149-150.

in the community at large. The progressive and dynamic ideals of Muhammadiyah, certainly, did appeal rather more strongly to the class of small traders to be found in urban centers and in rural market towns than it did to the peasantry, but there were many exceptions.[18] It might be more correct to speak, again with an eye to the exceptions, of an urban–rural opposition rather than a class opposition. Geertz[19] points to the two extremes—on the one hand a man who is old, rural, uneducated, and deeply pious is likely to be strongly conservative; and on the other hand a man who is young, urban and educated is likely to be modernist; but between the two extremes there are innumerable variations in the pattern. The political significance of twentieth-century variations in Indonesian Islam must be examined in the context of the more general twentieth-century situation. As a general judgment at this point, it may be said that the reformist movement represented a further attempt on the part of Islam to offer a unifying faith capable of coping with the problems of transition in the modern world and able to supplant the other distinct variants of the Indonesian cultural tradition. But in spite of its aspirations, Islamic modernism was still not to become a universal faith.

An Inspiration to Economic Development?

It remains to discuss one other aspect of Islam's role in Indonesia, which so far has merely been hinted at. The greater strength of the faith in the commercial centers of the country has raised certain interesting speculations in the minds of some modern observers about the possible economic contribution of religion. Reference has already been made to Geertz's comparison between Islam during the early days of its diffusion throughout the archipelago and Protestantism in Europe. The principle of equality of believers and the very austerity of the faith made it at least an appropriate religion for traders in the coastal principalities. Geertz went further and suggested that Islam played a more positive legitimating role, justifying and sacralizing commercial activity which, in the Hindu-Javanese view of the world was necessarily an inferior and ancillary function.

Stated in these terms the thesis may suggest some interesting corol-

---

[18] For a discussion of modernism's relations to urban traders, see W. F. Wertheim, *Indonesia's Society in Transition*, pp. 205ff.

[19] Geertz, *Religion of Java*, p. 163.

laries. If Islam was the handmaiden of trade in the fourteenth and fifteenth centuries, ought it not to have promoted the growth of a capitalist spirit, to have stimulated in time a greater flowering of Indonesia's commerce—and in due course, who knows, to have laid the foundations for an industrial revolution? That its initial economic influence was limited needs little explanation. Indonesian trade was curbed first by the Portuguese and later by the Dutch, who established a monopoly over much of the trade of the archipelago and so stifled the development of the indigenous commercial community.[20] Thus for centuries there was no opportunity for Islam's dynamic qualities to assert themselves. It might still be expected, nonetheless, that in the modern situation, with these limiting factors removed, the Islamic trader, whether in Java or outside it, would be the person most likely to offer leadership in meeting the current urgent problem of economic growth. The strength of Islam in the commercial areas of south Sulawesi and west Sumatra, together with the fact that in Java religious devotion tends to be strongest within the class of rural traders, may appear to support the expectation.[21]

There are obvious objections to this argument. The correlation between commerce and Islam is not a tight and close correlation, as we have seen. And even if it were it would not necessarily follow that Islam could offer the appropriate ideological support for modern economic development. Though it may have appealed to the earlier trading communities dotted along the trunk routes of Asia, it must be remembered that these communities were engaged in small-scale peddling on a precapitalist basis. There is no body of evidence in the history of other Moslem societies to suggest that the values of Islam are especially calculated to inspire its followers to greater economic efforts or to steel them for the task of economic revolution. And the modern class of petty traders in Indonesia does not, at least on the face of it, appear to be cut out for the role of dynamic and innovating entrepreneurial leadership. It is partly for this sort of reason that another observer, W. F. Wertheim, has felt inclined to challenge the Geertz argument. Wertheim advances the interesting hypothesis that the economic leadership of underdeveloped societies is more likely to be drawn from among the members of bureaucratic classes rather

[20] See, e.g., B. Higgins' Introduction to the Symposium *Entrepreneurship and Labour Skills in Indonesian Economic Development* (New Haven, 1961).

[21] Clifford Geertz, *The Religion of Java*, pp. 1-7.

than from the ranks of small traders.[22] He refers, for one of his examples, to the role of the samurai in providing appropriate values and active leadership for the task of Japanese industrialization, and he suggests that for Java "an ideology conducive to modern industrial growth . . . is much more likely to be developed among the modern representatives of the *priyayi* class" rather than by the *santri*. This is an interesting speculation, and some evidence for it may be found in the economic development of the Balinese court-centered towns where aristocratic elements have displayed decisive entrepreneurial characteristics.[23] In general, however, one wonders whether such a hypothesis has taken sufficient account of the *priyayi* inclination towards a static and contemplative view of the universe. Their emphasis on conceptual thinking seems to be poorly adapted to the task of economic innovation.

Whatever the theoretical merits of the two views the fact remains that, during the early years of Indonesian independence leading members of the Moslem community were among those with a coherent approach to the economic problems of the Republic. Men like Mohammad Natsir,[24] Mohammad Roem,[25] Sjafruddin Prawiranegara,[26] all members of the Masjumi party, were representative of able Moslem leadership and possessed a live sense of economic difficulties and of the problems of development. Masjumi's part in the first three cabinets of the Republic—the Natsir cabinet, the Sukiman cabinet and the Wilopo cabinet—gave promise of a serious approach to the tasks of independence. Whether or not the Moslem community in general possessed the necessary potentialities to play its part in a modern capitalist resurgence is another matter. As events turned out Masjumi was unable to preserve its initial political advantage. Its decline in the face of the gradual assertion of the bureaucratic values later to

[22] W. F. Wertheim, "Religious Bureaucracy and Economic growth" (paper presented at the Fifth World Congress of Sociology, Washington, 1962). Wertheim, in this paper, takes a slightly different view from that developed in Chapter 8 of his *Indonesian Society in Transition* (The Hague, 1956).

[23] See Geertz, *Peddlers and Princes* (Chicago, 1963), for a discussion of this role.

[24] Chairman of *Masjumi's* Executive Council, and Premier 1950-51.

[25] Foreign Secretary in the Natsir Cabinet, and Minister of the Interior in the Wilopo Cabinet of 1952-53.

[26] Finance Minister in the Hatta Cabinet of 1949-50, and in the Natsir Cabinet; subsequently Governor of the Bank of Indonesia until his flight to West Sumatra at the end of 1957 to take part in the subsequent rebellion as Prime Minister of the Government of the Revolutionary Republic of Indonesia.

be expressed in the President's theme of guided democracy may be seen, perhaps, as an example of the age-old tension between Java and the outer islands, between commerce and bureaucracy, to which reference has been made.[27]

The economic potentialities of Islam are thus still to be realized. In this sense as in others it remains merely one element in a complex of traditions.

[27] See below, Chapters FIVE and SEVEN, for a further discussion of this theme.

FOUR

Early European Influences

Sixteenth to Nineteenth Centuries

Indonesia's position on the fringe of a far-reaching international society, at once part of it and yet detached from it, receptive to external cultural influences but able in great measure to deal with them on her own terms, was not radically altered in the sixteenth and seventeenth centuries when western Europe established her direct and continuing contact with the world of Southeast Asia. The string of forts established by the Portuguese in Indonesian coastal areas in the sixteenth century and the rivalry of the British and Dutch East India Companies in Indonesian waters in the seventeenth, represented a new cultural tradition to be encountered, assessed, and made the subject of some kind of mutual accommodation. Nonetheless there were differences between this cultural encounter and those that had preceded it. The European came not merely as trader or priest or missionary but also as soldier, and the balance of material power was on his side. He was therefore able in the long run to determine the nature of the contact that was made. And whereas Indonesia had been able, in greater or less degree, to absorb and transform Hindu or Moslem influences, weaving them into the pattern of her own tradition, she tended, for as long as possible, to keep the European at arm's length, to see him as the bearer of a distinct and alien culture that could not be so readily absorbed.

This general judgment needs, perhaps, a little further discussion, for it touches on issues that have been debated a good deal in recent years. The question of whether the coming of the European represented a break in the continuity of Indonesian history has been raised already in these pages, but it is important enough to take up again briefly at this point. In van Leur's formulation of the question, based on his peddling trade theory, to which attention has been drawn, two separate though related questions need to be distinguished from each other: the question of whether or not the arrival of the European constituted a major watershed, and the question of whether the new forces became the determining forces in Indonesian history. The central element of van Leur's argument was that the Dutch East India Company's activities did not constitute a radical innovation in the trade of the Indies, but rather fitted into existing patterns. The Company was not a representative of a capitalist trade but was rather a merchant prince whose activities were comparable to those of the aristocrats or rulers whose occasional investment had supported the activities of peddlers from time immemorial. As a corollary to this argument it followed that the European did not seriously undermine the autonomy of Indonesian history during the seventeenth and eighteenth centuries. While the Company was at work, that is to say, it made merely a peripheral impact on Indonesian life and society, and the motive forces of Indonesian history continued to lie within Indonesia rather than outside it.

In developing the first of these lines of argument, van Leur, as we have seen, had a polemical aim in view. A sympathizer with the Indonesian nationalist movement and a passionate enemy of the self-glorification which was part of the "white man's burden" ideology, he was concerned to show that the heavy emphasis placed by some colonial historians on the role of the European in Asian history in general was misleading and inconsistent with the facts. His methodological apparatus—his redefinition of the concept of capitalism, for example—was fashioned for this purpose, and it was of great importance for his theme. As is so frequently the case with historical revisions, his contribution lay not in the discovery and presentation of new evidence but in the new insights that he brought to bear on the old evidence. However, as often happens when a controversial thesis is expounded, he tended to overstate his case in order to counter the overstatements of the opposition. There would be general agreement today with his argument that the arrival of Portuguese and Dutch did not constitute a dramatic break in the continuity of the history of Asian trade. There would be less general agreement with his implication that the arrival of the European represented almost no change at all. At the very least the Dutch East India Company was an organization of greater size and complexity and power than was to be found represented in the ranks of his peddlers. It was one organization, they were a swarm. It operated as a single concern across a greater distance. Its successful assertion of a monopoly was in itself a new element in the commerce of the area. It was able to mobilize greater force when the occasion demanded it. It is true that the Company for long tried to stand aside from the internal politics of the islands. It was concerned to take only such steps as were necessary to safeguard its commercial monopoly. It established its footholds in Java, in the Moluccas and Celebes, but apart from these enclaves its relations with Indonesian rulers were in a sense "international relations" rather than the relations of a suzerain to its dependants.[1] Nonetheless as time passed it was drawn more and more into dynastic disputes and more and more its intervention gave it territorial interests, so that, at least in Java, it became heir to the indigenous authority of Mataram and Bantam.

Both politically and commercially then, while the appearance of European trade in the archipelago did not mark a rapid and sudden turning point in Indonesia's history, it was certainly to be followed by gradual changes of considerable significance in the nature of Indonesian trade and in the character of political authority in the islands. Hall's judgment strikes the right balance:

. . . from the point of view of South-East Asia the Dutch triumph over the English is to be seen as the first decisive step towards the formation of a new empire, commercial at the outset like Srivijaya and Malacca, but gradually becoming predominantly territorial; yet not in the true line of succession to either, since the centre of control lay thousands of miles away.[2]

At the same time it must be admitted that the significance of the Portuguese capture of Malacca in 1511, or of the Dutch victory in their struggle for dominance over the British East India Company in the early seventeenth century, was of small moment when compared

---

[1] The exact nature of Dutch suzerainty is an involved question. For a discussion see G. J. Resink, " 'Inlandsche Staten in den Oosterschen Archipel' (1873-1915)," and J. M. van der Kroef, "On the Sovereignty of Indonesian States: a rejoinder," in *Bijdragen tot de Taal-, Land-, en Volkenkunde*, Vols. 116 (1960) and 117 (1961) respectively.

[2] D. G. Hall, *History of South-East Asia* (London, 1955), p. 251.

with the much greater impact to be made by the Netherlands toward the end of the nineteenth century. The direct investment of private Dutch capital in the Indies, the growth of a plantation system dependent upon Indonesian labor, the shift of economic interest from Java to Sumatra, and the extension of political control, hitherto based firmly only in Java and at a few scattered coastal points elsewhere, over the outer islands—all of these nineteenth-century developments represented the imposition of a new economy and the creation of a new political unity. They also stimulated social change at a speed and of a magnitude unseen during the previous two-and-a-half centuries of Dutch contact. If there is a real watershed, a dramatic break in the continuity of Indonesian history, it falls in the nineteenth century rather than in the sixteenth or the seventeenth century.

This point leads us to the distinct but related question which worried van Leur—the question of the autonomy of Indonesian history. In rejecting the traditional periodization of Indonesian history—Hindu-Javanese, Islam, the colonial period—and in arguing his case for continuity after 1600, van Leur was also arguing that the Dutch did not disturb in any fundamental way the pattern of authority of the society with which they were dealing. The motive forces of Indonesian history continued to come from within.[3] In the seventeenth century "the Oriental element, not the colonial, was dominant." [4] In the eighteenth century Dutch influence in Java was increasing, but elsewhere the threads of control were fragile—"a few European centres of power had been consolidated on a very limited scale"—but in general "the Oriental lands continued to form active factors in the course of events as valid entities, militarily, economically and politically." [5] The test of this judgment is a test of power—"what was the power—political, maritime, economic—of the harbour principalities" [6] and van Leur's assessment of the evidence led him to the view that even to the beginning of the nineteenth century Indonesian history retained its own autonomous development and its own equality

[3] The question of the periodization of Indonesian history, and the question of which element is dominant at which period, is discussed specifically in three reviews by van Leur of successive volumes of F. W. Stapel ed., *History of the Netherlands Indies*. The reviews have been republished in *Indonesia Trade and Society*, pp. 249ff.

[4] *Ibid.*, p. 262.
[5] *Ibid.*, p. 274.
[6] *Ibid.*, p. 276.

against the separate development of the European civilization that was impinging on it. But this was not to continue. Till then

> Two equal civilizations were developing separately from each other, the Asian in every way superior quantitatively.

> Equality remained as long as the magic poison of modern capitalism had not yet enchanted Europe and northeastern America to produce steam, mechanics, and grooved cannons.[7]

With industrial revolution in Europe it would seem that even van Leur was unable to deny a point of departure after which external pressures became more important than Indonesian factors in determining the shape of developments in the islands.

This point is not made specifically by van Leur. It is merely hinted at. In his thorough examination of van Leur's whole theme, John Smail[8] takes up the point and argues that van Leur had no need to falter even for the nineteenth century. To the test of independent power as a criterion for autonomy Smail adds the test of cultural independence (a test that van Leur sometimes implies but never specifically distinguishes from the power criterion). If the historian places his emphasis on underlying social structure, or culture in the broad sense rather than on relative strength, then the whole question of the autonomy of Indonesia will take on a new light, says Smail, and the antithesis between the Europe-centric and the Asia-centric view will be transcended. The Indonesian elite may have become too weak by the nineteenth century to resist the continuing pressure of the foreigner, but the society of which that elite was a part retained its vitality. Dutch power in the later years of their empire has dazzled us so that we have failed to see how shallow this rule really was, how vigorous indigenous society really remained, and how the changes which admittedly occurred within it were really just adaptations made, or accepted, by that society itself as it kept up with the times.

In developing this argument Smail draws attention to the need for a closer study of the history of individual ethnic groups within Indonesia. (His own illustration suggests the way in which an autonomous history of Atjeh might be written with its central theme relating to

---

[7] *Ibid.*, p. 285.

[8] John R. W. Smail, "On the Possibility of an Autonomous History of Modern Southeast Asia," *Journal Southeast Asian History*, Vol. 2, No. 2 (July 1961). See also Harry J. Benda, "The Structure of Southeast Asian History: Some Preliminary Observations," *Journal Southeast Asian History*, Vol. 3, No. 1 (March 1962).

a conflict between *adat* leaders and Islamic leaders, and with the Dutch merely impinging on this internal conflict.) The implications of such an approach do, however, extend beyond the recommending of local histories and they suggest the possibility of dealing with the colonial relationship itself, not as the dominant theme of Indonesian history even during the later colonial period, but as a sort of "foreign relations" theme in Indonesian (as also in Dutch) history. Thus, in summary, to overcome the problem of a Europe-centric perspective it is not enough to give the "other side of the story." It is necessary to tell a different story—a story centered on social and cultural changes rather than political ones. To do this one must overcome two barriers —the barrier posed by the conventional view of Indonesian society as enfeebled and disrupted by the Dutch, and the further barrier posed by the common preoccupation of Dutch and Indonesians alike with the colonial relationship. If these barriers are removed, the colonial relationship will assume its proper position as merely a part of the story and the indigenous society will be seen to possess its own strength and adaptability. The way will thus be open for a truly autonomous history of Indonesia.

Smail's argument is an ingenious one. Nevertheless his case has some of the hallmarks of a tour de force about it, and one wonders whether he does escape from van Leur's problem—whether indeed he is really concerned with the same problem. His search for autonomy is accompanied by a desire to establish an essential continuity in Indonesian history and an attempt to play down the elements of discontinuity. But it is precisely the turning points—the periods of accelerated change and of new departures—that tend to catch the interest of historians. Van Leur was concerned to shift the watershed from the sixteenth to the nineteenth century, but he did recognize a different temper in the late nineteenth-century story—a difference that is apparent whether one is concerned merely with relative strengths of Dutch and Indonesians or whether one is concerned with profounder currents of social change. Smail does not deny the greater importance of Dutch influence at the close of the nineteenth century, nor does he deny the magnitude of social change in this later colonial period. But in his concern to insist that these developments need not impair the concept of autonomy, he does minimize change and emphasize continuity. Such phrases as that the Western powers in Southeast Asia were no more than "a thin layer resting on top of large and essentially intact societies" [9] or that in Indonesia social structure remained coherent while going through "a certain amount of change" [10] do minimize developments which historians may properly be concerned to stress.

We have given fairly close attention to this debate, for it is an important one for contemporary studies of Indonesia, and it is essential to clarify the main issues. At the end, however, while recognizing the importance of approaching Indonesian history on its own terms, it is reasonable, in dealing with that history after 1600, to recognize at least two main divisions. While Portuguese and early Dutch commercial activities have been much more a continuation of existing patterns of trade than has often been supposed, it is still possible to observe important changes that followed the successful establishment of the Dutch monopoly. Second, it is important to stress the acceleration of change that occurred toward the end of the nineteenth century. That acceleration was an inescapable and important fact, whether one is focusing attention upon economic developments, upon shifts in political authority or upon changing configurations within the society as a whole. It will be convenient, then, to accept 1870 as the approximate point of division in our examination of Indonesia's adjustment to the presence of the European in each of these three spheres.

Superficial Contacts and a Trade Monopoly

The coming of the European made little immediate difference to the general economy of the islands. In Java an intensive cultivation based on a complex irrigation system remained the basis of agriculture after 1500 as before. And the same sort of broad judgment may be applied also to the *ladang* cultivation of the outer islands. Insofar as the archipelago was subjected to the pressure of new economic interests during the sixteenth, seventeenth, and eighteenth centuries, the effect was felt primarily in the field of external trade and not in that of domestic agriculture. First under the Company and then under the State, Holland applied alternative methods to the collection and export of products—cloves, nutmeg, pepper, coffee, and sugar in particular—for which there was a European market.

The important economic innovation resulting from the establish-

[9] Smail, *op. cit.*, p. 101.
[10] *Ibid.*, p. 90.

ment of a Dutch foothold in the islands was the monopoly of trade.[11] In the closing years of the sixteenth century Dutch and English traders had begun to invade the preserves of the Portuguese in the East. From the outset the Dutch were present in greater numbers, and a series of Dutch companies was formed after 1594 to finance voyages to the East. In 1603 the British East India Company received its charter, and its first voyage resulted in the setting up of a factory at Bantam—a move that played a part in persuading the Dutch, in their turn, to combine their own efforts. In 1602 the Netherlands' United East India Company, Vereenigde Oostindische Compagnie (V.O.C.), was formed and became the instrument by which the Netherlands, in succeeding years, was able to exclude all European rivals from the trade of the archipelago. The collapse of the Company at the end of the eighteenth century brought the Crown directly into the picture, and after the interregnum of the Napoleonic Wars, the State itself became responsible in its own way for the control and conduct of the trade. But the general principle remained unchanged. The methods of Company and State represented successive ways of exploiting in a mercantile way the resources of the Indies. And their effects upon the indigenous economy were similar. They led to the crystallization of a dichotomy between a mercantile economy on the one hand and a primarily subsistence economy on the other. They were instrumental in destroying the flourishing Javanese trading class that had grown up in the harbor principalities during the preceding centuries. If the Dutch were creating a new Srivijaya as Hall suggests, they were doing so as an external elite. The total result, then, was an isolation of the Indonesian economy from the direct contacts with an extensive international trade in which it had participated hitherto.

The Company's methods of creating this monopoly lay through the establishment of scattered footholds that could serve as centers of its collecting operations and also as focal points of its power. Away from these factories its trading methods fitted closely into a traditional mold.

It carried on trade at the many trading points everywhere in the archipelago in the same way as Oriental traders and on the same footing, buying cloves on Ambon from the Ambonese *orang kaya* in his house,

---

[11] Monopoly, of course was a matter of degree. See Kristof Glamann, *Dutch-Asiatic Trade, 1620-1740* (Copenhagen and The Hague, 1958), which throws doubt on the completeness of the Company's monopoly.

on the scales of the nobleman, as the Javanese trader did; buying peppei in Jambi alongside the Chinese small engrossers from men come down from Minangkabau, buying on no larger a scale than the Jambi court lords and the Javanese, Malay, and Chinese traders coming there. In Achin . . . it was subjected to the imposition of a toll by the *panglima* just the same as everyone else.[12]

But the factories grew in importance as the Company's role began to surpass that of other traders and as it began to elbow them out of the way. Jan Pieterszoon Coen, as the governor general of the Indies from 1618 to 1629, laid the foundations of a future commercial empire from which the Netherlands could not easily retreat even had she had any desire to do so. Partly by the direct use of force and partly by treaty with native rulers, he consolidated the V.O.C.'s position against the rival British East India Company. He was drawn into successful military action against Sultan Agung of Mataram. And he established Batavia as the headquarters of Dutch operations. His successors extended the network of trading posts that enabled monopoly to be completed.

To the mere collection of Indonesian products was added, in the course of the eighteenth century the principle of forced deliveries of crops, a policy of exploitation that could be applied only in regions under the direct control of the Company, and which, in effect, represented a demand for tribute not so totally different from that which Indonesian rulers had themselves imposed upon their subjects. This new policy was accompanied by the introduction of new crops— coffee in particular—which were added to those already of interest to the Company. But from the point of view of the local economy this added pressure did not constitute a genuine economic stimulus. Tribute was merely tribute. In paying it the producer was not brought into direct contact with an outside market, but merely with an overlord.

When the State took over the affairs of the Company at the end of the eighteenth century, there was little substantial change in this situation. During the British interregnum of 1811-1816, certainly, there were some departures in policy, such as the introduction of money taxes to replace forced deliveries, but these changes were radically modified after the Netherlands returned, at the end of the Napoleonic Wars, to the control of its former possession, and especially after 1830 when Van Den Bosch introduced the Culture System in Java. This

---

[12] Van Leur, "On the Study of Indonesian History," *Indonesian Trade and Society*, pp. 149-150.

system involved exacting the produce from one fifth of a peasant's land in lieu of tax. This was in fact a more formalized and more thoroughgoing version of the forced deliveries system of the eighteenth century. The culture system, like its predecessor, did result in the production of new crops—sugar, coffee, and tea in particular—and in the expansion of the area devoted to the production of exports. Partly because of this it made possible a rapid growth of population. It also meant that the government made a more forceful and penetrating impact on the economy of the village than had been the case in the days of forced deliveries or earlier when tribute was paid to Indonesian rulers. Its demands were greater and in consequence it involved a direct encroachment on rice lands and the imposition of new and heavier demands on labor; in these respects it marked a change from the past and represented a new and distinct phase of Dutch economic policy. But it was still essentially a tribute system nonetheless, whose impact on the indigenous economy was an external impact, and as such it was calculated to prevent the Javanese villager from producing for the world market in his own right.[13] The producer was not himself drawn into the wider economy for which the products were destined, nor was he given any incentive to expand production or to develop new techniques. The important thing in Dutch eyes was to preserve, by monopoly, a high price at home but a low price for the actual producer in the Indies. In economic terms, therefore, the Dutch, in the first 250 years of their contact with the Indies, achieved no technological revolution but concerned themselves with the collection of Eastern produce in increasingly forceful fashion but still in such a way as to perpetuate the division between a subsistence agriculture on the one hand and the world of trade on the other.

Increasing Dutch Involvement

There were shifts in political authority in the islands over the same two and a half centuries, as Indonesian principalities sought to adjust

[13] The most recent and most illuminating treatment of the character of the Culture System as a means of deriving agricultural products from the Indies without changing fundamentally the structure of the indigenous economy is to be found in Clifford Geertz, *Agricultural Involution: The Process of Ecological Change in Indonesia* (Berkeley and Los Angeles, 1963), Chapter 4. An important analysis of the continuing function of the landrent system within the Culture System is given by R. van Niel, "The Function of Landrent under the Cultivation System in Java," *The Journal of Asian Studies*, Vol. 23, No. 3 (May 1964).

themselves to the gradual intensification of Dutch economic pressure, but once again, except in a comparatively small area, these stopped short of the establishment of the complete and direct control the Netherlands was to achieve in the closing years of the nineteenth century and the opening years of the twentieth. Some existing states did come under the direct control of the Company. In others there was merely an erosion of power as Indonesian princes succumbed to the new pressure. The decay of royal authority enabled the Company gradually to inherit the princes' authority without making it necessary for it to reshape the actual process of government. To that extent Indonesia's patchwork of political systems was able to survive and to a degree to absorb the Company as a new political force within the existing political order.

The Company itself deliberately sought to avoid territorial responsibilities. Its object was trade not only within the archipelago but in mainland Southeast Asia as well, and its commercial purposes were best served by the capture of control over sea routes, not by the establishment of a territorial empire. The Dutch capture of Malacca (1641) and the assertion of control over Ceylon effectively terminated Portuguese influence. And in the Indies themselves maritime power, buttressed by a series of fortified footholds through the islands, was necessary to secure the desired monopoly of trade. Beyond that any expansion was seen as involving quite unwarranted expense.

It proved impossible, however, from the beginning to preserve a stable balance between the Company and the existing powers of the Indies or to confine the former to dominion merely over the seas. Local rulers in the vicinity of Dutch factories were inevitably drawn into a special relationship with the Company. Princes sought its help on occasion to deal with restless subjects and would-be princes sought its help over disputed claims to succession. Able to exercise power in this way the Company acquired, almost accidentally, a few areas of continuing authority where it acted at first as a kind of suzerain and later as something more than that. In the Banda islands and the Moluccas, in Ternate, and Amboina trading rights were gradually converted into effective political control. But these were still only footholds. In Java the process went further. Mataram's clash with the Company in the 1620s was followed by a period of peaceful coexistence. But twenty years later an internal rebellion in Mataram evoked Company intervention and the upshot was to reduce the throne of that kingdom to a position of dependence on Dutch power.

A similar intervention followed in the state of Bantam. In return for support to Mataram's ruler, Holland acquired the cession of a large slice of her territory including the Preanger region in the mountains southeast of Batavia. This territorial nibbling represented a first step toward the creation of a genuine empire. It was to be followed by others. Through a series of wars of succession one pretender to the throne of Mataram after another bought Dutch support by further cessions of territory and, by the end of the eighteenth century, practically the whole of Java had come under the Company's control. The once powerful kingdom of Mataram was divided in 1755 into two small principalities—Surakarta and Jogjakarta—which were to survive as reminders of an earlier glory until Dutch rule itself was ended. Its disintegration had sprung partly from internal causes and to that extent was parallel to the type of collapse its predecessors had suffered from time to time over the preceding centuries. But one important contributing factor in this case was the pressure of an alien commercial power able to extend its sway as that of Mataram contracted.

By the end of the eighteenth century the Dutch had inherited the authority of Mataram and Bantam in most of Java. But they were still not anxious to establish a thorough administrative control beyond what was necessary for commercial purposes. The Company's position in Java and outside it was that of paramount power, not of ruler. The transition from this type of authority to the creation of a more formal and systematic political control was a gradual business. After the Dutch government had succeeded the Company, Daendels, as governor general during the Napoleonic Wars, began to fashion a more thoroughgoing system of administrative divisions through which the authority of Batavia could be exerted. His work was carried further during the brief period of British rule in Java when Raffles introduced his land rent system as a means of abolishing the tribute character of forced deliveries. Economically Raffles' system had insufficient opportunity to prove itself before it was reversed, but in political terms it involved the establishment of a closer contact between a central administration and the traditional authorities of Javanese society.[14] The trend was intensified after the restoration of Dutch power, particularly after 1830 when Van Den Bosch's Culture System brought its own need for a thorough and systematic administration.

[14] J. S. Bastin, *The Native Policies of Sir Stamford Raffles* (Oxford, 1957).

But even these administrative reforms were based in broad outline on the methods of territorial control which had been used by Mataram itself and by its predecessors. A hierarchy of divisions manned by "officials" of varying degree bridged the gap between court and village. The term "officials" is, perhaps, misleading, suggesting as it does the existence of a formalized bureaucracy. The officials of the Javanese kingdoms were rather petty rulers who had been brought under the control of a king as he extended his power outward from his capital. They retained a considerable degree of autonomy over their areas—how much depended on their nearness to the capital, the effectiveness of communications, and the power of the particular monarch—but they were nonetheless caught up in the tribute system of the kingdom and came in time to occupy a position more closely resembling that of an official class, removable by the ruler, and rewarded for loyalty by the assignment of a proportion of the produce derived from their region.[15] Java never produced a landed aristocracy but rather an aristocracy of officials. As the Dutch came to demand, through forced deliveries and later through the Culture System, the diversion of the island's agricultural surplus to themselves rather than to the traditional servants of traditional authorities, it became necessary for them to convert this class into a salaried bureaucracy. The Company, and later the government of the Netherlands, thus stepped, by gradual stages, into the shoes of Mataram and Bantam. The main change in fact, as time passed, was merely a growing formalization and intensification, rather than a real change in the character of the system itself.

With the demands of the Culture System, however, the degree of formalization was, perhaps, sufficient to be considered a change in kind, and not merely in degree. The kingpin of this system was the regent, who now was given high station and high pecuniary reward but who lost much of his independence and was brought into a position of direct allegiance to the Dutch officials above him. Through the regent and the lower officials responsible to him the government's control over the village from which produce was drawn became a more efficiently conducted affair. By the end of the Culture System the outlines of the later territorial administrative hierarchy were apparent. At the top of the pyramid Dutch residents were responsible

[15] See B. J. O. Schrieke, "The Native Rulers," in *Indonesian Sociological Studies*, I (The Hague, 1955), for a discussion of the process whereby "ministeriales" were transformed into civil servants.

for coordinating the tasks of government in territorial divisions termed residencies. Residencies were composed of a group of regencies and in each a Dutch *controlleur* preserved contact with, advised, and to some extent supervised the Indonesian regent. The *controlleur* represented the point of contact between European and Indonesian bureaucracy. Below the regent and responsible to him were Indonesian district officers and sub-district officers who manned the lower territorial divisions into which the regency in turn was divided. At the bottom of the pyramid, the sub-district officer maintained the vital link between official and village, between government and governed. This pattern, developed in Java, was to be elaborated in greater detail as Dutch authority consolidated itself more thoroughly toward the end of the century, but the main features were determined by the mid-nineteenth century. As Furnivall said, "the framework of administration looked much the same in 1850 as in 1830; but it was constructed on a different principle, and with steel instead of bamboo."[16]

These developments were indeed important innovations. Though the new administrative system followed the main outlines of a traditional pattern, they involved a clear change in the character of traditional authority. The regents, in accepting the overlordship of the Dutch, were bound to the service of an alien power. They were rewarded in some degree for their loyalty. Backed by Dutch authority they were more secure in their position as an aristocratic class than had been the case in the past when custom had placed clear limits upon them, and when the peasantry had possessed its own means of resisting or evading the demands of oppressive rulers. By a constitutional regulation of 1854 the position of regent itself was made hereditary. At the same time the regents lost much of the independence they previously possessed, and became very fully identified with alien rule.

Outside Java several different patterns of administration developed. As Dutch authority was extended to more parts of Sumatra during the course of the nineteenth century, a system of direct rule was instituted which followed the Javanese pattern fairly closely except that the European bureaucracy penetrated to one level further down the hierarchy. But in other parts of the archipelago the more common pattern was one of indirect rule. Recognition was extended to exist-

[16] J. S. Furnivall, *Netherlands India: A Study of Plural Economy* (Cambridge, 1939), p. 122.

ing rulers who were bound to the Dutch by a form of treaty whereby they agreed to accept the authority of the government in Batavia but, in return, were left with the forms of power and with a good deal of independence in the internal administration of their principalities.[17]

This is to anticipate a little. There were no Netherlands East Indies in the full sense even by the mid-nineteenth century; as will be seen, the major extension of control was to come after 1870. At the beginning of the century, the whole position of the Netherlands in the Indies was fluid and there was not even a clear definition of spheres of interest between herself and Britain. At the end of the Napoleonic Wars and the British interregnum in the Indies, the Netherlands received back Java and Malacca, while Britain retained Penang and Bencoolen, and acquired shortly afterwards the island of Singapore. The map was made to look tidier in 1824 by an Anglo-Dutch treaty in which Malacca was exchanged for Bencoolen. Sumatra was thereafter regarded, by a vague understanding, as falling within a Dutch sphere of interest while the Peninsula fell within a British sphere. Even so it was to be some time before this division between spheres of interest became effective as a division between empires. The full expansion on both sides of the Strait of Malacca came after 1870.

Shifts in the Balance of Indonesian Society

Just as the Indonesian political order showed a considerable degree of resilience but was nonetheless eroded gradually by Dutch pressure, so the social order of the islands was able to preserve its main outlines while some important changes were beginning to occur beneath the surface.

Again the process was a gradual one. In the seventeenth and eighteenth centuries Indonesian societies were able to face the new European arrivals with a dignity and an assurance born in many cases of their own refinement and sophistication and reflecting a confidence in their own tradition. As long as the Company's interests

---

[17] Two forms of agreement were used. The "Long Contract," designed to cover the Netherlands' dealings with fairly substantial rulers, specified in some detail the relationship that was to exist between a ruler and the Dutch. Toward the close of the nineteenth century, the more summary "Short Declaration" provided merely for a recognition of Dutch sovereignty, a renunciation of the right of a state to conduct its own foreign affairs, and an agreement to accept regulations prescribed by the Netherlands for internal administration. This more blanket form of submission was applied to the large number of small states that were then being brought under Dutch control.

were essentially commercial, there was no need for either the inland kingdom of Mataram or the coastal powers of Java, Sumatra, and the eastern islands to feel any sense of inferiority to the newcomer. And even after it had begun to acquire political authority, its control was not such as to disrupt the values and organization of traditional culture. It offered no alternative way of life or set of values that could compete with the traditional norms of a native aristocracy. In Java the Company, in inheriting the authority of Mataram in many areas, superimposed itself upon the existing administrative organization of that state and commanded the services of existing officers. But the courts of Mataram, and after 1755 of Jogjakarta and Surakarta, remained for those officers the center of society and the model for a refined and civilized way of life. And from the point of view of the commoner the change of overlord did not really affect the character of the village. If a social adjustment was made in this meeting of cultures it was made quite as much by the Dutch, who fitted themselves into the Indonesian scene to a remarkable degree. They adopted for themselves "the opulent life of the higher classes in the Indies, with their country seats, their pomp and ceremony, their retinue of slaves and serfs—a life linked to that of the Javanese nobility more than to any other." [18] Certainly Batavia in many respects must have reflected the desire of the Dutch to bring a little bit of Holland with them. Its canals and its "stuffy, tightly packed, many-storied houses," says Wertheim,[19] did perhaps represent an attempt to build a faithful copy of Amsterdam. But within a short time these houses became breeding grounds of disease, and the Dutch began to affect a more luxurious style of life, more feudal in its outward appearances and consciously adapting itself to that of the Javanese aristocracy. One has only to observe one survival of old Batavia—the building which has now become the National Archives of the Republic—to find an architectural example of the life of the Company's servants. With its spacious rooms and its extensive quarters at the rear for a retinue of servants, it represents a style that contrasts both with the original attempt to export a Dutch town to the Indies and with the suburban products of a later age to be seen in Menteng or Pegangsaan.

There was one aspect of the Company's policy, however, that was to have important social consequences for the future, namely the

---

[18] Van Leur, "Three Reviews," loc. cit., p. 286.
[19] W. F. Wertheim, *Indonesian Society in Transition* (The Hague, 1956), pp. 170-73.

patronage extended to the Chinese. Chinese traders, like those of other Asian countries, had participated in Indonesia's trade long before the arrival of the European and they had established themselves in small numbers in the coastal cities. The Company drew them from these enclaves and found a place for them in the interstices of its own economic structure. They were useful as collectors of the products in which the Company was interested, and in this capacity they provided an alternative to the more usual reliance upon the Indonesian aristocracy. In some instances villages were actually leased to Chinese, who, in return for a fixed delivery to the Company, were permitted to extort for themselves as much additional produce as they felt they safely could. Under the aegis of the Company the foundations were laid for the dominant position the Chinese later came to assume in the retail trade of the islands, and for their less enviable position as a highly distinct minority within Indonesian society. Already in the days of the Company, the Chinese were to a considerable extent a distinct group. They neither merged into the society around them nor stimulated any radical change in that society.

It was not until the increasing Dutch pressure of the nineteenth century that significant shifts in the internal balance of Java's social organization began to occur. It was the thoroughgoing character of the Culture System, economically and administratively, that altered the character of aristocracy and village alike. The administrative streamlining required for the intensive exploitation of Java's land and labor meant formalizing what had previously been a loosely organized hierarchy of local rulers, and this had the effect of separating them in some important respects from the society to which they belonged. Their powers, formerly defined by custom, were now derived from the strength of an alien government, and their interests thus tended to be bound to those of their new masters. Similarly within the villages themselves, the demands of the new tribute system had its consequences for the customary pattern of authority. The village headman, like the regent above him, was made responsible for the collection of produce required for delivery to the government and his position as a representative of the semi-autonomous village was complicated by this new function—the function almost of a servant of a higher authority. Below the headman the pressure of government often tended to break down traditional distinction between nuclear villagers—those who held land—and those of lower rank.[20] These processes had probably begun to operate as a result of the contingencies and freed deliveries of the Company in the eighteenth century, but they were confirmed and accelerated in marked degree in the nineteenth century.

Outside Java Dutch administrative pressure was less except in a few narrowly restricted spots such as Ambon, Makassar, and Minahasa. In these areas the Company had asserted its monopoly, sometimes by extremely drastic measures (the destruction of clove crops for example), but since they had been centers of trade before the days of the Company, the subjection to Dutch control had involved them in a change of overlord but not in any profound economic or social revolution. In west Sumatra, certainly, Dutch support of *adat* leaders in the Padri wars did have much the same effect on traditional authority as was the case with the *priyayi* of Java. As in Java this was a case of the inland extension of Dutch power and of the maintenance of forced cultivation, and it was the exception to the normal pattern as far as the outer islands were concerned. In these areas for the most part it was not until the end of the nineteenth century that the expansion of Dutch territorial control began to shape itself into genuine empire, with a deeper and firmer administrative control and with consequent changes in social patterns.

By the third quarter of the nineteenth century, then, most of Indonesia was merely on the threshold of genuine colonial subjection. The foundations of empire had been firmly laid only in Java, and even there the economic and social consequences, while significant, had stopped short of being revolutionary. Population had certainly grown rapidly under the Culture System. Numbers in Java had increased from 6 million to 9.5 million but this was not the product of any technological change. The expansion of Javanese agriculture had been what J. H. Boeke called "static expansion"—the straightforward extension of established techniques to hitherto uncultivated areas. In the process the dichotomy in the Indonesian economy, to which we have referred—cultivation being in Indonesian hands and collecting and marketing in the hands of foreigners—was hardened and confirmed. The Javanese cultivator did not receive the profits from the sale of his produce and had neither opportunity nor incentive to enter a wider economy.

[20] Wertheim, *op. cit.*, p. 140.

This seclusion was not a new thing. The peasant had contributed his produce to the support of his rulers before this. But the scope of the export economy was new. Company and government in succession had extended the range and volume of the archipelago's involvement in the world economy, while Indonesia's society remained based still in a largely subsistence labor-intensive agriculture. It was later to be the boast of the Dutch, that, in their government of the islands, they had disturbed existing social patterns very little. The claim itself was a dubious one, as we shall see in greater detail. Even before 1870 there were significant changes in the balance of village society and in the character of supra-village authority. But insofar as Dutch policy in fact had succeeded in protecting indigenous society from the shocks of culture contact, one might well wonder whether, on balance, the net result was beneficial. A different policy might have enabled embryo entrepreneurial tendencies to express themselves and might thus have made it possible for Indonesian agriculture to begin the difficult process of transition into the modern world from which, in fact, it was sheltered.

At the level of ideas and of values a similar dichotomy existed. Indonesia in spite of its proved ability to adopt and absorb cultural influences from outside found little that was attractive in European civilization during the first two-and-a-half centuries of contact with the Dutch. And the Dutch, for their part, were not yet interested in making an ideological impact upon the society of the Indies. There was thus a sharpness of opposition in the meeting of Indonesia and Western Europe which had been absent in her earlier encounters.

Europe was, in time, to make an ideological challenge, but only after there had occurred a switch in the character of the Netherlands' economic and political interest in the area. After 1870, but more particularly after 1900, the Netherlands was to bring a more positive dynamic into her policy. It remained to be seen whether that dynamic was sufficient to make possible a new cultural integration.

FIVE

DUTCH EMPIRE IN THE INDIES

1870-1942

Between 1870 and 1930 the exports of the Indies increased from 107 million guilders to 1,160 million guilders.[1] Their character changed also. Whereas in 1870 the area's main contribution to a European market was in the form of coffee, sugar, tobacco, together with the garden products of the eastern islands—mace, cloves, nutmeg, and pepper—by 1930 the balance had changed entirely and industrial products had come to the fore. Rubber, despite world overproduction and the price fluctuations of the 1920s, was exported in 1930 to the value of 173 million guilders and oil to the value of 190 million guilders. Copra and tin were important additions also. Exports of sugar and tea increased absolutely during the same period, but their relative importance declined sharply.[2]

This economic expansion brought about a shift of interest from Java to Sumatra—the new estate production had taken place to a considerable extent in Sumatra's East Coast Residency—and it was accompanied by a further extension of political authority not merely over Sumatra but over the outer islands in general. Sumatra itself had been the subject of a gradually increasing penetration in the decades before 1870. Bencoolen was acquired from Britain in 1824 (in exchange for Malacca), and Palembang was brought under control in 1825. The principalities of the northeast coast—Siak, Deli, Serdang, Langkat, and Asahan—accepted Dutch authority by treaty in 1858. At about the same time moves were made to extend control

---

[1] J. S. Furnivall, *Netherlands India* (Cambridge, 1939), pp. 207, 336.
[2] *Ibid.*, p. 337.

over the Batak areas, though this task was not completed until later. Djambi and Atjeh posed more serious problems. Atjeh indeed presented the Dutch with their most difficult proposition and involved them in a long-drawn-out war lasting from 1873 until resistance was finally overcome in 1908. But while considerable Dutch effort was devoted to the subjection of Atjeh, rapid advances were made in the remainder of the outer islands. In Borneo, Celebes, the Moluccas, and the Lesser Sundas, areas which had already accepted a general Dutch overlordship were brought more firmly under administrative control, and the same control was extended to new areas. Under the governorship of Van Heutsz,[3] in particular, principality after principality accepted the authority of Batavia, so that by 1910 the final shape of the Netherlands East Indies was practically completed. In 1906 the submission of Bone and Luwu brought south and central Celebes under control. In the Moluccas, Ceram and Buru were controlled by 1907. Ternate came under firm control in 1909. In Borneo a similar forward movement could be observed, and even in New Guinea between 1898 and 1901 officers were stationed at Manokwari, Fakfak and Merauke. Space does not allow a complete list of important additions during these years, but these few names may indicate the magnitude and despatch of the whole operation.[4]

In their spread and scope these developments were revolutionary. After two-and-a-half centuries of comparative quiescence during which the Dutch had established themselves firmly only in Java, and even there without promoting fundamental changes in the structure of society, their forward movement had almost an explosive character. The change in tempo was not the product solely of changes in Dutch policy. It was part of a much more general movement of expansion on the part of Western Europe as a whole. The release of European expansive energies on the economic basis of a century of industrialization constitutes one of history's most remarkable phenomena. During this comparatively brief period Britain, France, Germany, and Italy scrambled for Africa, for special privileges of investment in the Far East, and for the partition of the South Pacific. In Southeast Asia the British forward movement in Malaya brought the Peninsula

[3] J. B. van Heutsz, in charge of operations in Atjeh until 1904 and governor-general from 1904 to 1909.

[4] See E. S. de Klerck, *History of the Netherlands East Indies*, 2 vols. (Rotterdam, 1938) for a fuller account.

under control between 1874 and 1914. The Netherlands' expansion from Java to the outer islands formed part of the same process.

To some recent observers this process represented, in fact, the creation of modern Indonesia—the imposition of an effective unity, the laying of the foundations of a modern economy and the radical alteration of traditional social patterns. Indonesia's nationalists in due course came to look back to the unity imposed by Madjapahit as the forerunner of the modern nation, but whatever one makes of Madjapahit's claim to suzerainty over areas outside Java, Madura and Bali, the old east-Java-based empire clearly never had anything like the political and administrative control that the Dutch imposed upon the archipelago in the early twentieth century. Whether one wishes to praise or condemn the colonial period there is some truth in this view of its creative role. At the same time, the changes of the period were never sufficient to obscure the persistence of older traditions.

The motive force lying behind the new imperialism in Indonesia was that of private capital seeking an entry to the economy of the Indies and a share of the profits hitherto monopolized by the government. By 1870, the pressure of private investors in Holland had secured the adoption of a new Agrarian Law that permitted private entrepreneurs to acquire land under lease from Indonesians or from the government, and the liberal policy—"liberal" in the classical laissez-faire sense—was under way. (The Culture System was not thereby abolished; it lingered on for some decades but was of declining importance.)[5]

Since the object of the liberal policy was still the export of Indonesia's products, principally agricultural products, to a West European market, it might be argued that it was merely a new device for achieving an old well-established goal—that it replaced the Culture System just as the Culture System had replaced the contingencies and forced deliveries of the Company. This view is taken by Clifford Geertz, who regarded the system not as a fundamentally new development but merely as one of a series of techniques for implementing "more or less the same program"—a program designed "to pry agricultural products out of the archipelago, and particularly out of Java, which were saleable on world markets without changing funda-

[5] See Furnivall, *op. cit.*, p. 336, for figures showing the increasing proportion that privately produced exports bore to the total exports of the Indies after 1870.

mentally the structure of the indigenous economy." [6] Like the Company system and the Culture System before it, the liberal system was another method by which the European side of Indonesia's dual economy "was to be more efficiently organized for the production and marketing of export crops." [7] But to state the argument so strongly is to ignore fundamental differences in the organization of production and indeed in the whole character of the new economy that was created. Whereas the products collected under the Culture System and before were grown by agriculturists working on their own land and still within the framework of a traditional organization, the direct investment of Dutch capital created a new form—the plantation— geared to the production of industrial rather than garden products. The plantation system as it developed in Indonesia was a matter of corporative enterprise, the plantation itself being in the hands of a salaried estate manager employed by a company based in the Netherlands rather than the Indies. Though a system of large scale business, however, it was not heavily capitalized by the standards of contemporary Europe and made its profits largely because of the cheapness of the land and the labor available to it. Estates were concentrated primarily in Java and in northern Sumatra where the environs of Medan were transformed by a concentrated and spectacular network of plantations into an example of economic geography quite unlike anything else in Indonesia.

In one respect, however, the liberal policy can be regarded as a continuation of earlier policies and this is the nub of Geertz' comparison. To a considerable extent it confirmed the exclusion of the Indonesian from direct contact with external trade. This consequence was certainly not foreseen by liberal theorists. The liberals shared the optimism of contemporary economic theory, which, in the colonial as in the domestic field, saw an automatic connection between economic development and welfare. The maximizing of wealth, it was held, would inevitably produce a maximizing of welfare without the necessity for more positive action by the State. Indeed economic laws being what they were, any interference with them, it was believed, would have the reverse effect: it would upset their perfect operation and would therefore tell against welfare in the long run. Applied to the economy of the Indies this theory held that, given

---

[6] Clifford Geertz, *Agricultural Involution: The Process of Ecological Change in Indonesia* (Berkeley and Los Angeles, 1963), p. 47.

[7] *Ibid.*, p. 50.

minimum safeguards to redress the unequal bargaining position of the Indonesian, the free play of economic motives would stimulate a general economic development in which Indonesia as well as the Netherlands would ultimately share. The minimum safeguards were embodied in the 1870 Agrarian Law,[8] which confirmed existing customary rights over land, prevented the alienation of Indonesian land and confined the activities of the European investor to leasehold land, with the responsibility placed on the Government to see that land necessary for the subsistence of the Indonesian was not leased. Further safeguards were embodied in labor legislation that provided for the recruitment of Indonesians, but which imposed checks to see that the recruit understood the nature of the contract, and that he was granted minimum wages and conditions of work.[9] Beyond these restrictions it was an article of faith that the energies of private enterprise would provide an example to the Indonesian and would stimulate his participation in the wider economy to which he was now introduced. The facts, however, did not fulfill the expectations of the theory. The expansion of European estates, and the development of new wealth thereby, did not lead to comparable advances in Indonesian well-being or to Indonesian participation. Despite the rapid increase in production reflected in the growing volume of exports from the Indies, there was a falling per capita income and much social and cultural dislocation. By the 1890s a rising tide of criticism in the Netherlands demanded specific action to meet the problem.

Wishful Visions

There were marked differences of opinion as to how to better the Indonesians' lot. It was recognized that the economic strides of the liberal policy had produced great social upheaval, but on the question of whether social change should be encouraged, the official attitude was ambivalent and to some extent self-contradictory. It sought at once to promote social change and to retard it—to transform the indigenous social order and to preserve it. On the one hand humani-

[8] See J. S. Furnivall, *op. cit.*, pp. 178ff.

[9] The Coolie Ordinance of 1880, which applied only to recruitment for the East Coast Residency of Sumatra, was not as extensive as this. It provided for registration of contracts before an official, but apart from that its main purpose, reflected in the penal sanction that was applied to laborers who neglected their work or deserted, was to give the employer almost complete control of the laborer. Later legislation determined minimum wages and introduced more rigorous supervision of the system.

tarians were concerned at the fact that the removal of restrictions of Dutch capital had led to a decline rather than to an increase of welfare for the individual Indonesian, and they emphasized the need to protect native society from the disruption that necessarily accompanied direct investment, the employment of Indonesian labor, the taking up of land, and the extension of a money economy. On the other hand there were those who stressed more positively the responsibility of the Netherlands to redress such damage as she had wrought by the introduction of a positive policy of planned economic development for the Indonesian, aimed particularly at the village level. In so doing she would, in effect, be fostering and controlling the direction of social change instead of allowing it to take place in a haphazard fashion.

These were, no doubt, contradictory goals, though each in its own way was an example of Dutch policy at its noblest—and also at its most mistaken.

The first of these two attitudes was given clear expression at the very end of Dutch rule by the last of her proconsuls, Lt. Governor General Hubertus J. van Mook.[10] The whole system of government, said van Mook, had been intended to preserve Indonesia's customs and civilization.

> The protection of the village and the small independent farmer was one of its principles; customary law was generally maintained, and since 1870 no non-Indonesian has been allowed to acquire a title on Indonesian-owned land; the absence of large estates worked by tenant farmers was a result of this policy. The native civil service and the organization of the native states were objects of constant care; the supervision of the elections of village headmen laid its stress on character and capability.

Whether the ideal was realized quite as fully as van Mook suggests is a matter of doubt. Some observers thought that it had been. Even J. S. Furnivall, who was a critical observer of Dutch rule, considered that the "scrupulous care for the preservation of customary law, the restrictions on the alienation of village land to foreigners, and the tradition of abstaining from intervening in village affairs seem on the whole to have been effectual in protecting the village

---

[10] H. J. van Mook, *The Stakes of Democracy in South East Asia* (London, 1950), p. 108.

community against the solvent influence of economic forces." [11] As far as the village was concerned "Dutch rule has, in great measure, been successful in softening the impact of the modern west on native social life." [12]

In making this general judgment Furnivall was not blind to important changes which had taken place. Even under the Culture System, as we have already seen, the demands of government on the village had impaired the internal balance of forces within the village and had altered the nature of the authority to which the village was traditionally subject. Under the liberal system the forces of change were accentuated. The village continued to be protected in many ways, but a large number of people were drawn out of the villages into the cities or on to the estates. The villages themselves in some areas—in sugar-growing areas in Java for example—were brought into the orbit of the market economy. The Agrarian Law and the Coolie Ordinance, to which reference has been made, imposed some degree of control on the operation of Dutch capital, but they represented minimum measures only. They protected the individual Indonesian to some extent in his relations with Dutch business. They did not protect the society from which the individual came. At the level of government and administration efforts were indeed made to base authority on traditional forms. Indonesian aristocrats continued to be used in the lower levels of administration in the directly ruled areas of Java. But these officials had far less power than prestige or wealth and so were in a bad position to shelter the society they helped to rule. In the outer islands the tremendous territorial expansion of the period was made mainly on the basis of agreement with existing rulers who submitted to the authority of Batavia but were left comparatively free to order the domestic affairs of their principalities. This type of indirect rule, it was held, constituted a buffer between the alien rulers and their Indonesian subjects. In fact, insofar as there was a buffer, it was created by distance and isolation rather than by political forms. Isolated regions—regions that fell outside the sphere of Dutch economic interests—were left fairly undisturbed. Others felt the currents of change even if they remained nominally under their traditional sovereigns. In general the official picture of a society

[11] J. S. Furnivall, *Colonial Policy and Practice: A Comparative Study of Burma and Netherlands India* (Cambridge, 1948), p. 263.
[12] *Ibid.*

insulated from the disturbing effects of Dutch economic pressure was a highly idealized one.

Those who held the second point of view—that which urged the positive promotion of change—could argue that it was in any case impossible to wall off Indonesia from the modern world. Their views were based chiefly on a deliberate and self-conscious humanitarianism. In 1899 an expression of this humanitarianism was given by C. Th. van Deventer[13] in his idea of an "honor debt." Holland, it was argued, had drained wealth from the Indies during the Culture System and was in honor bound to repay this—by contributions from the Dutch Treasury to assist the colony's finances and to promote Indonesia's welfare. This idea was to have an early opportunity of implementation. In 1901 a combination of Christian and Social Democrat criticism of the Liberal government, then in power in the Netherlands, brought about its fall and enabled the application of van Deventer's principles in what came to be known as the Ethical Policy. Financial assistance from Holland was to assist agricultural development and would provide health and education services for the local population. At the village level agricultural extension programs would help to stimulate the economy. Above the village level the provision of Western education for the elite would supply the administrative and technical skills that were lacking. In this way Indonesian society would be brought into the mainstream of progress.

In proposing a policy of expenditure from the home treasury, the Netherlands was many years ahead of other colonial powers. It was not all sheer altruism, admittedly. The extension of educational facilities in particular had its selfish aspects. With the expansion of government responsibility and the activities of private business there was a need for clerical and technical assistance in the lower ranks of government and business administration which could most cheaply and conveniently be met from the local population. But it would be unjust to characterize the Ethical Policy as a whole in terms of Dutch self-interest. A genuine strain of idealism was present in van Deventer's appeal for action, in the view of his supporters in Holland, in the ranks of officials in the Indies whose job it was to secure the practical application of the policy. In form and intention it anticipated by a number of years the sort of colonial welfare policy that

[13] A graduate of Leiden, van Deventer followed a legal career in Indonesia by service as Liberal/Democrat member of the States General.

other Europeans were later to implement in their own territories.[14]

If the earlier Liberals had shown a naïve nineteenth-century optimism in believing that capital investment in the tropics would be
attended automatically by countless benefits for their inhabitants,
the exponents of the Ethical Policy were equally optimistic. They
foresaw no particular problems in the way of economic, social, and
political advance beyond those of finance and guidance. Guidance
would be supplied by a benevolent administrative service whose members would push through developmental schemes by the use of
"gentle pressure" since a degree of mild coercion was necessary to
overcome the conservatism of tradition. The provision of finance
was to be the direct responsibility of the Netherlands. "Money—that
is the indispensable oil with which the Indies machine will have to
be lubricated before it can be got over the dead point." [15]

The provision of welfare at the level of the village and above it,
and the promotion, in general, of economic development, did not,
however, exhaust the intentions of the Ethical Policy at least as conceived by some of its supporters. These were means rather than ends.
Beyond such aims was a more distant and more all-embracing goal:
the creation of a new society for the Indies, and, on the basis of the
new society, a new political order as well. The Netherlands, in brief,
was embarking on an attempt to direct the course of change on a
vast scale. On the political level the provision of facilities for higher
education for a limited number of Indonesians—at first only for those
of higher birth but later for others also—was seen as a contribution
to long-range plans for conceding to the colony some measure of control over its own affairs. The precise degree and character of such
self-government was never defined in detail, but some sort of special
relationship seems to have been envisaged between the Netherlands
and a semi-autonomous Indonesia. This involved, in turn, a multi
racial partnership in the Indies themselves since the Netherlands
clearly did not intend to withdraw either her economic interests or

[14] Cf., *e.g.*, Britain's Development and Welfare Policy, elaborated in a White
Paper in 1940 and embodied in the *Colonial Development and Welfare Act* of
that year. Like the Ethical Policy, the Act was based on the principle that finan
cial assistance from the metropolitan taxpayer should be devoted to the introduction of productive and welfare schemes for colonial populations.

[15] C. Th. van Deventer, "A Compromise Proposal," quoted in part under the
title "A Welfare Policy for the Indies," in *Indonesian Economics* (The Hague,
1961), pp. 256-262.

her nationals from the colony. According to one formulation the proper consequence of the Ethical Policy would be the gradual emergence of a new society—East Indian society—neither Western nor Eastern but containing elements of each: a modern society able to contend with the pressures of the modern world but drawing its cultural strength both from traditional Indonesian sources and from the West.[16]

This sort of concept reflected one of the most fundamental facts about the Netherlands' feeling for her colony. Dutchmen in Netherlands India, unlike Englishmen in India or West Africa, regarded the islands as genuinely their home. They did not find it absolutely necessary to send their children to Europe for their education. They did not themselves invariably plan to return home upon their own retirement. Many of them certainly followed this kind of expatriate pattern. But for many others, though the Netherlands was the object of an occasional visit, the Indies were their home. They brought their wives and maintained their families. They built towns, many of which attempted to reproduce little bits of Holland in the tropics. As Wertheim says, they created a society modelled on less expansive lines than that which the Company's servants had built, and they lived more in the style of a prosperous bourgeoisie.[17] The large houses had given way to suburban villas, though built still in a substantial style. These facts conditioned much of the thinking about the ultimate goals of policy. Seeing themselves as a permanent factor in the Indies, the Dutch were forced to grapple with the problems of the sort of relationship that could be maintained between themselves and

[16] One version of this view may be found in A. D. A. De Kat Angelino, *Colonial Policy*, II (abridged trans. by G. J. Renier in collaboration with the author, The Hague, 1931). In Chap. 4, De Kat Angelino distinguishes between the situation in European countries, where the State is the product of society, and that in the East, where society is divided into innumerable "small and isolated genealogical, territorial, or functional communities." "In these circumstances Western state organization is compelled to call forth social consciousness and forces and to develop from the tens of thousands of isolated communities that wide and lofty social sphere from which in normal circumstances it would itself have been born. The state is thus engaged in calling into existence its unborn mother, the society that fits it." Dutch rule through Indonesian officers and rulers provides "the steel structure of unity." Education, economic development, communications assist in unifying and modernizing. The same developments will enable the cooperation of European, Chinese, and Indonesian. The racial groups will retain their own racial identities but will play their part in the one society. Only when this is achieved can political independence be granted.

[17] Wertheim, *op. cit.*, p. 180.

Indonesian society. And the concept of "East Indian society," based on some form of partnership, and enjoying considerable autonomy, was for many a nobler goal than that of ultimate independence for the colony and complete separation from the Netherlands.

The outlines of this vision were left vague. It was never made clear, for example, whether it aimed at the assimilation of the Indonesian to Western civilization, or at the "association" within the one political entity of diverse traditions.[18] Both approaches found supporters. There were those who held that both Islam and *adat* were enemies of progress. If the people of the islands were to enter the modern world, they would have to acquire the economic orientations of the West and for this they would need to accept the dynamic attitudes to life which were characteristic of the West. This goal was to be achieved primarily through education, aimed first at the well-born who would be ready to recognize Western superiority and able to learn Western ways of thought, and extending gradually to the population in general.[19] Others, however, were less sure of the superiority of Western civilization, or recognized more clearly the subtle complexities and pitfalls of cultural change, or, more positively, rejected the implied disparagement of Indonesian culture and considered it worth preserving for its own sake.[20] This school of thought was more cautious in its expectations and, though still desiring change, was anxious in the short run to protect village society, and, even in the long run, to preserve a diversity of cultures in the archipelago.

While the distinction between these two approaches might be considered a matter of emphasis, the former view—that which saw westernization rather than mere modernization as the key to Indonesia's future—represented a new ideological challenge to traditional culture. As we have seen, the Dutch, throughout their earlier years of contact with the Indies, had offered no such alternative ethos, no integrating point of view to bind diverse elements into a unity. In this respect Europe had had less to offer than had earlier influences

[18] For a discussion of the distinction between assimilation and association see Robert van Niel, *The Emergence of the Modern Indonesian Elite* (The Hague, 1960), pp. 36ff.

[19] For a discussion of this type of approach, represented particularly in Snouck Hurgronje, see Harry J. Benda, *op. cit.*, pp. 20-31.

[20] The difference between the two approaches was to be observed particularly in legal theory. How far should the Netherlands aim at establishing a single legal system or how far should *adat* law be allowed a continuing recognition?

from Asia. The Dutch had adapted themselves in great measure to the Indonesian scene rather than the reverse. But late-nineteenth-century confidence had introduced a new tone to the contact between East and West. There was a missionary element, an element of cultural imperialism, which had been lacking before. "But how glorious is the aim that we pursue!" said van Deventer.[21] "It is: the formation out there in the Far East of a social entity which is indebted to the Netherlands for its prosperity and higher Culture, and thankfully recognizes this fact."

The grand design of the Ethical Policy reflected the easy, self-confident and indeed arrogant optimism of industrial Europe at the turn of the century. It failed to take into account the toughness and coherence of other societies or to recognize the complicated character of social change. It assumed too easily that change could be channelled and directed. Certainly new forces were set in motion during this period and some of them were indeed released by the policies pursued under the Ethical Policy. But they took unexpected turns and expressed themselves in unexpected ways. The positive aims of the policy were, in their own way, as unrealistic as were the efforts to soften the impact of new economic forces. If the Dutch in their most enlightened moments were anxious at once to promote change in some directions and to retard it in others, they were to be doubly disappointed, for events themselves took charge.

Paternalism in Action

One consequence of the drive for welfare was an enormous increase in the scope and intensity of government. Since the State was accepting the positive duty of developing native society, some increase in its activities was, of course, inevitable. For government had not merely to find the finance for the new program; it had also to supply the necessary administrative supervision. The prosecution of agricultural extension schemes through which new knowledge could be brought to the village, the building of new roads to break down isolation, the extension of irrigation works, the erection of new schools and clinics, all required the paternal oversight of a new class of government servants. The lower ranks of the territorial administrative service continued to be staffed by Indonesians, and the Ethical Policy

---

[21] Quoted in van Niel, *op. cit.*, p. 38.

further intensified the trend, already noticed, for regents, district officers and sub-district officers to acquire greater power over the people of their domains and to become more firmly identified with the alien government. In addition to an increase in the role of these traditional figures there was a closer supervision by the European members who staffed the upper ranks of the service, and there was also in process of creation a new bureaucracy to staff the technical services of government.[22] The result was a much deeper penetration of government into the crevices of village life. The Indonesian became aware as never before of an alien power standing behind the indigenous officers with whom he had immediate contact. And, in spite of the genuine benevolence which undoubtedly lay behind some of the actions of government, the Indonesian's response was not one of gratitude for what was being done for him. He was able to identify government as the source of new taxes and new pressure as well as of welfare. He resented the efforts demanded of him supposedly in his own interests. Even though the coercion used to implement welfare policies was usually softly applied by "gentle pressure," the villager was still reluctant to perform a variety of tasks which had not seemed necessary to his forefathers. The Dutch may have been concerned to create a welfare state. Primarily they succeeded in creating simply a state—a power whose presence was felt by all of its subjects.

What in fact did the new policy achieve? Most of the contributions made to the Indonesian economy under the Ethical Policy were in the nature of palliatives. They provided some alleviation of particular areas of hardship, but they did not achieve—and they did not attempt to achieve—any thoroughgoing technological changes. In spite of the expectations of some supporters of the Ethical Policy, the benevolence of the Netherlands and of the Indies government did not extend to the point of envisaging any far-reaching alterations

[22] The distinction between the territorial service and the technical services of government was, and is, an important one. Members of the territorial service staffed the divisions and subdivisions of the country—provinces, residencies, regencies, etc.—and the territorial service as a whole formed a vertical chain of authority from the center to the remotest village. Its task was, in general, to govern—a task that included coordination, at each administrative level, of the activities of the technical or functional services, health, agriculture, works, etc. The territorial service was an elite service, based in part on traditional patterns of authority. The functional service sprang into existence as the Indies acquired, after 1900, some of the appurtenances of a modern state.

in the economic order which had been established by Dutch capital during the preceding thirty years. The large Dutch firms and corporations were to remain the principal agents of development. For the Indonesian sector of the economy, agricultural extension programs enabled the improvement and extension of irrigation, the cultivation of new land, and the introduction of new crops. Improved credit facilities eased the burden of indebtedness. New communications offered wider opportunities of commercial contact. But these improvements served merely to check the fall in living standards as population grew. They stopped far short of providing any real stimulus to the latent forces of economic enterprise that might exist within village society. A glance at the kind of practical program envisaged by the planners of the Ethical Policy reveals no intention to bring about a technological revolution. Education, irrigation, emigration formed the basis of their three-pronged approach to progress, and the latter two, particularly, were seen as a sufficient solution to the problems of population growth and rural poverty.[23]

In education rather more revolutionary goals were contemplated. Education in the eyes of the modernizers was to be the agency through which the offerings of Western civilization would be made available to the Indonesian, and provision was made not merely for the extension of primary education but for the provision also of secondary and higher education, either in the Indies or in Holland itself, for a more select elite. But in this field, too, actual achievement was pitifully small. By the eve of World War II, Holland had achieved a literacy rate for Indonesia of about 6 per cent.[24] In the middle ranges of education only a handful of graduates was produced annually.[25] Those able to secure a university training were more limited still in number. The failure of the Netherlands to train an adequate reservoir of indigenous trained technicians and administrators may be regarded as one of the major failures of her colonial policy.

[23] See, e.g., A. W. Idenburg, Minister for the Colonies, quoted in van Niel, op. cit., pp. 32-33.

[24] The 1930 census gave a figure of 6.44%. It should be noted, however, that this figure was calculated on the basis of the total population, including children. It has been argued that if children below the age of ten were excluded from the calculation, the figure would be 30.83%. See S. L. van der Wal, Some information on Education in Indonesia up to 1942 (The Hague, 1960), p. 7.

[25] George McT. Kahin, Nationalism and Revolution in Indonesia (Ithaca, 1952), pp. 31-32.

Thirty years of Ethical Policy, then, did not arrest declining welfare or prepare a solid foundation for social change. The limited character of the policy's achievements was to be underscored further in the early 1930s when depression affected the export sector of the economy and laborers displaced from the plantations returned to put increasing pressure on the village. At the same time, it must be recognized that, despite the failures of official policy, the period of the Ethical System was nevertheless a period of quite dramatic change in which dynamic forces were released. These developments were in part the by-products of policy—the uncontrolled and unexpected consequences of measures which had been aimed at a different goal. In part they stemmed from causes quite outside the sphere of government actions and intentions.[26]

The expansion in the all-pervasiveness of government to which reference has been made may be placed in the first category. So may the long-term consequences of the government's education policy. In comparative terms those who had been able to avail themselves of the new educational opportunities may have been few, but the results of the policy were out of all proportion to the number directly affected. The Netherlands, in effect, took steps to create an educated elite without giving proper consideration to the problem of how its members were to be employed. In consequence she created an important and vocal class of discontented people and contributed enormously to the intellectual ferment of Indonesia's awakening and nationalism. The new elite was drawn both from aristocratic ranks and from lower social levels. Under the influence of Western education, these people became detached in great measure from the framework of their own tradition and were representative rather of a new urban culture. Individual ethnic loyalties were weakened. New patterns of behavior were adopted suited to the suburban life of the principal cities. There were opportunities for some of these people in the ranks of administration, whether government or business. But for all practical purposes such openings were available only at the middle and lower levels. The virtual reservation of higher positions for Dutchmen was, in itself, a cause of resentment. This was accentuated by the further fact that there were insufficient places even in

---

[26] For a consideration of the extent to which change was undirected and unexpected, see W. F. Wertheim and The Siauw Giap "Social Change in Java 1900-1930," *Pacific Affairs*, Vol. XXXV, No. 3 (Fall 1962).

the lower reaches of the system to absorb all those who had received a Western education. Thus the educational policy of the Ethical System, so far from contributing to the emergence of an integrated East Indian society, had produced an unemployed class of emotionally displaced persons.

Significant as were these consequences of the Netherlands' welfare policy, they were overshadowed by the more profound disturbances following inevitably from the general economic development of the period. The mere fact of private investment, and of the plantation economy it created, brought a host of changes in its train. The growth of the necessary financial and commercial services for the new economy—banks, business headquarters, export houses, the growth of port facilities, and the extension of a network of internal communications, the development of a limited—a very limited—degree of industrialization, and the expansion of retail trade transformed such towns as Batavia or Surabaja or Medan into modern commercial cities. The population increase of the period helped to swell the size of the cities as a new class of unaccommodated persons, detached from village society, sought openings for unskilled employment. The process of urbanization was productive of social problems of a variety of kinds. The overcrowded urban kampongs lacked adequate sanitary provision and they multiplied slum-like conditions in the major cities. More important, perhaps, than their physical shortcomings were their deficiences as social organisms: they did, in some measure, seek to recreate in a new setting the communal patterns of the rural village, but obviously they could not attain the same degree of cohesion, and their inhabitants were therefore uprooted people, no longer enfolded within a stable pattern of rights and obligations. Their growth was a part of an accelerated process of social dislocation. The same process saw the emergence of new skill groups, though of a low order, minor mechanics, chauffeurs and the like, as Indonesians were drawn into the service of the European commercial economy. All of these things were the consequence of a rapidly expanding capitalist economy. As Benda says, "the tides of change . . . were running faster than ever before, but they were to all intents and purposes spilling over the banks charted by the proponents of the Ethical Policy." [27]

The rural scene was protected to some extent from these forces,

[27] *The Crescent and the Rising Sun*, p. 36.

but even here the changes of the period had their eroding effects.[28] The village was brought to some degree within the orbit of a money economy and this process played its part in weakening the values of tradition. So did the labor demands that followed the Coolie Ordinance and later labor legislation. Though only a small minority of villagers were drawn into the systematic organization of the indentured labor system, the effect of their recruitment was out of all proportion to the numbers involved. The Indonesian who was removed from the environment of the village and brought under the alien discipline of the plantation was no longer surrounded by the obligations and restraints of custom. At the expiry of his contract he returned to his village bringing his new experience and his accumulated earnings with him, and was not able to fit easily back into his old niche. Nor was the village easily able to absorb him. These forces of change were thus disruptive rather than creative. At least they were not able to propel the traditional economy along the path of development. Small country towns were important crucibles of change, and here there were more hopeful signs of creative adaption. Usually the administrative headquarters of regency, district or sub-district, with official residences and government offices grouped about a central square, such towns were also commercial centers with their street of Chinese shops but with the presence of an indigenous trading community as well. The activities of the Indonesian trader were centered on the town market place, and his function was usually to maintain a link between the Chinese merchant and the surrounding rural population; but in finding a place for himself within an economic system still dominated by foreigners, he might be regarded as the possible representative of a gradual institutional change which could conceivably, in due course, allow the release of new economic energies. But in the meantime the economic dominance of the foreigner was the important thing and the indigenous class of petty traders had little opportunity to emerge as the pioneers of an economic revolution.

"Dual Economy"

The proponents of the Ethical Policy, at their more optimistic moments did, of course, set their sights too high. The kind of transforma-

[28] D. H. Burger's study of structural changes in Javanese society, published in *Indonesië* between 1948 and 1950, is important. Part of the study has been translated under the titles *Structural Changes in Javanese Society: The Village Sphere* and *Structural Changes in Javanese Society: The Supra-Village Sphere* by the Cornell Modern Indonesia Project, 1956 and 1957.

tion that some of them envisaged was on an impossible scale. More-over they lacked an appreciation of the theoretical problems of eco-nomic growth. It was not surprising therefore that their policy failed to achieve a controlled economic and social development but had the effect rather of creating or strengthening divisive tendencies within indigenous society.

To assess the nature of these divisions is a task of some complexity. It may be useful at this point therefore to turn from a descriptive account of policy and its consequences to a consideration of some of the analytical devices that observers have used in their examination of Indonesian society as it had developed by the closing years of Dutch Empire. A convenient point of departure is offered by one analysis of the Indonesian situation that enjoyed considerable popularity in Holland—the theory of economic dualism. When the liberal policy had failed to secure the permanent maximization of wealth and of welfare in the Indies, some critics began to insist upon the inade-quacy of liberal theory to prescribe for the Indonesian situation. Clas-sical economic theory, it was argued, might have applied well enough to homogeneous West European industrial society, but did not fit Eastern societies. A new and distinctive theoretical approach was therefore needed, and this was found in the concept of the "dual" character of the Netherlands Indies' economy.

The theory of dualism is both illuminating and a little perverse. Its most elaborate formulation was developed by J. H. Boeke,[29] who argued that, by its very nature, Asian society posed special problems to economic development and, in consequence, made what he de-scribed as a dualistic situation inevitable. Boeke drew attention in broad and dramatic terms to the contrast between the modern econ-omy of plantations, import-export houses, banks, and all the apparatus of large-scale commerce that had grown up under Dutch control on the one hand, and, on the other, the conservative, traditional, largely subsistence economy based on the village. The latter depended on primitive techniques and it was integrally connected with a whole traditional social order—a society in which, it was held, the dead hand of custom inhibited the proper play of economic motives and thus stood in the way of economic development. The contrast between the

[29] For one statement of Boeke's theme, see his *The Structure of the Netherlands Indian Economy* (New York, 1942). See also *Indonesian Economics* (The Hague, 1961), which gives a number of samples of Boeke's views together with samples of Dutch criticisms of it.

two economies was therefore a necessary feature of the colonial situation.

In drawing attention to this contrast Boeke toyed with several ways of posing the antithesis; between urban and rural economies, between East and West, and between native and foreign.[30] None of these formulations appeared satisfactory. The first antithesis—that between town and village, between world market and village economy—was blurred by the fact that estate development was non-urban, but still belonged unquestionably to the capitalistic side rather than to the precapitalist, village side of the antithesis. The other two classifications were rejected because some of the indigenous people had entered the capitalist sector of the economy, and, of course, the commercial role of the Chinese community cut across the East–West antithesis in any case. Further, the ending of the colonial tie would not have changed the dualistic character of Eastern societies once it had been created. Boeke was therefore forced to content himself with the formulation of a purely economic antithesis—that between an indigenous "precapitalism" and capitalism proper imported from outside. The former was held, in spite of exceptions, to be characteristic of Eastern Societies.[31]

Having made the broad distinction, Boeke's main concern was to elaborate it in greater detail and to insist that "precapitalism" in its Asian sense was not an earlier stage of development which, in due course, might evolve in a progressive direction, but was a totally different economic order which could not be analyzed in terms of classical economics. Precapitalism was grounded in a social environment which was hostile to economic growth. The Eastern village, he argued, was "primarily a social and religious unit" where economic motives as normally understood, did not operate. This view was based on a distinction which he felt to be fundamental to his whole system—that between economic and social needs. This distinction was elaborated in his first work on colonial economics, his doctoral thesis for the University of Leiden, in 1910. Economic needs were those needs felt by man as a separate individual. They were the sort of needs that underlay the concept of economic man. Social needs on the other hand "find their origin in norms set by the social collectivity" [32] and

<hr>

[30] Boeke, The Structure of the Netherlands Indian Economy, Chap. 1.
[31] Ibid.
[32] Boeke, Tropical-Colonial Economics, extract quoted in Indonesian Economics, pp. 69-70.

these norms often formed a major barrier to economic advancement. First of all, duties necessary for the preservation of communal solidarity obviously ran counter to that personal acquisitiveness which, in Western theory, provided the spur to progress. Though "every person in need . . . can count on help . . . the advantage of this is offset by a disadvantage . . . every prosperous person has to share his wealth right and left; every little windfall must be distributed without delay." [33] As a later observer has put it "shared poverty" rather than the pursuit of individual self-interest is the hallmark of village economic activity. Secondly the need to propitiate gods or spirits represented for Boeke another type of barrier to the emergence of economic man. The customary obligations imposed on the villager for this purpose did not lead to the gratification of felt needs even in the sense of providing inner satisfaction. They were simply ritual obligations. Tradition in its various forms thus created such a powerful resistance to change as to render almost hopeless the prospect of economic development. The duality of the economy was not due simply to the colonial relationship. Nor did it represent a meeting of different stages of development which would iron themselves out in time as the underdeveloped sector of the economy was subjected to the stimulus of western capital and western norms. As seen through Boeke's pessimistic eyes it was likely to be a permanent characteristic. The static character of traditional society was at worst a part of its very nature, and at best so firmly grounded that change was almost impossibly difficult and painful.

There is a seductive appeal about Boeke's thesis. By focusing a shaft of light on a central feature of the Indonesian scene, it appeared to illuminate the surrounding areas. It offered an organizing principle in terms of which a whole series of uncomfortable facts seemed to fall naturally into place. On closer inspection, however, his claim to be fashioning a really new theoretical concept was a dubious one, and the concept itself has its flaws. Three criticisms, in particular, may be levelled against the system. The theory was less distinctive than its exponents would have claimed; it oversimplified and also exaggerated the gap between the two sides of the dual economy; and insofar as such a gap did exist the theory overemphasized the extent to which dualism was a specifically eastern phenomenon.

The central point of the thesis—the recognition of the fact that

[33] Boeke, *Structure*, p. 25.

problems of economic development must be seen in their social context—is a truism, as applicable to Western capitalist society as to that of Netherlands India. And this was apparent enough to the Western "orthodox" economists whose theoretical approach was condemned by Boeke. The "ideal types" of the classical economist may have been regarded at one time as descriptive of the real world, but, by the time of Boeke's contribution, economists were ready enough to recognize the sociological factors within which their subject must be set. Once that recognition has been made a good deal of the individuality of Boeke's analysis disappears. Orthodox theory, having made the appropriate sociological assumptions, may be as applicable to an Eastern as to a Western situation.[34] Second, it would seem that the contrast between the capitalist and the precapitalist sectors of the Indonesian economy was overdrawn. As Boeke's critics have been quick to point out, even the Indonesian peasant has shown that he is not confined solely within a framework of socially defined wants. He is ready and willing to consume a wide variety of import goods when he has the wherewithal to do so. In modern Borneo, as Benjamin Higgins puts it, "good rubber prices result in a spate of orders for bicycles, mattresses, watches, fountain pens, and the like. Sampans in the remotest canals are loaded with Australian tinned milk and American tinned soup." [35] And other examples abound of limitless wants, which indeed, have come to pose problems of foreign exchange control to Indonesia's governments of today. Smallholders' rubber in Sumatra and Borneo, or copra in Sulawesi have offered plenty of evidence, during the colonial period and after, of the existence of an entrepeneurial spirit. A reservoir of mobile labor for employment in capitalist enterprise was a further clear consequence of western development after 1870. All of these facts would seem to reveal a much greater diversity in the Indonesian economy than Boeke was willing to admit. There were many degrees of difference to blur the contrast

---

[34] This view was argued against Boeke by many of his Dutch contemporaries, as the volume *Indonesian Economics* makes clear. A more recent and perhaps more trenchant criticism is that of Benjamin Higgins "The 'Dualistic Theory' of under-developed areas," *Ekonomi Dan Keuangan Indonesia* (February 1955; reprinted in *Economic Development and Cultural Change*, IV, January 1956). See also "Southeast Asian Society: Dual or Multiple" by Manning Nash, and "Comments" by Benjamin Higgins in *Journal of Asian Studies*, Vol. XXIII, No. 3 (May 1964).

[35] Higgins, *loc. cit.*, p. 63.

between the two sides of the dual economy.[36] Finally insofar as the contrast could be observed between more advanced and less advanced sectors, it was not a contrast whose existence distinguished Eastern from Western economies. Such differences could be observed in varying degrees in Western as well as Eastern situations. The simplicity of Boeke's classification is therefore misleading.

Having admitted these criticisms, however, it should be added that even a truism is worth restating from time to time. Duality is very much a matter of degree whether in Western or Eastern societies and, even if it should not be complete in a country like Indonesia, it is still true that the concept of dualism does seem particularly compelling there. In spite of the signs of economic motive and of commercial instinct which do exist, and which existed during the colonial period, it remains the case that the division between the export economy created by Dutch investment after 1870 and the "native" economy is, in broad terms, a genuine one. It may not require a distinctive economy theory to explain it, but it is there. The Indonesian was not completely excluded from the world market that the Dutch estates were created to serve. But he was excluded to a marked degree. The energies of the great mass of the population continued to be absorbed by a traditional agriculture using traditional techniques and extending only to a limited degree beyond a subsistence level.

There were some changes, it is true, in the "native sector" of the economy to match the growth of the "European sector" during the last seventy years of the colonial period, but they were not in any sense parallel changes. They were changes of elaboration of the existing system, not the introduction of a new one. Geertz uses the term "involution" to describe the *sawah* economy in its later stages from the culture system onwards. Improvements in irrigation techniques, themselves the result of Dutch initiative, had enabled the system of wet rice cultivation to prolong itself in the face of population growth, to avoid an economic revolution that otherwise might have been im-

---

[36] See for instance the argument of Clifford Geertz in his *The Social Context of Economic Change* (1956) that lack of a capitalist spirit was a consequence rather than a cause of dualism. The segregation of the Indonesian social structure from the effects of Western enterprise was a matter of deliberate Dutch policy. Geertz, taking his example from sugar planting in East Java, insists that this development did tend to stimulate Indonesian enterprise, but that the protection of the village, the exercise of Dutch control over all stages of production, and the policy of growing sugar by peasant labor, all helped to dampen the new stimulus that the development should have provided.

posed upon it, and to preserve, in exaggerated form as it were, the essentials of its traditional character.

The changes which, over the centuries, had occurred in Indonesian agricultural techniques had not been labor-saving but rather labor-absorbing innovations. Irrigation itself, in replacing a "slash and burn" economy, increased the number of man hours needed to work a given unit of land, and further changes—in tenancy, for example—accentuated that trend. The whole effect was the application of more and more labor and the more and more intensive cultivation of land. In theory there were limits to such intensification within the framework of indigenous technology. "At this point—one at which land runs out and per capita income begins to fall due to a fall in the marginal productivity of labour—one would perhaps expect either another revolution in the forms of land use (which would imply a revolution in social outlook as well) or a stabilization of population growth." [37] Neither of these things in fact happened because, says Geertz, the introduction by the Dutch of new crops, new tools, improved methods of irrigation, postponed the evil day. Instead of stimulating a dramatic agrarian revolution, therefore, the Dutch impact during the Culture System and after enabled native agriculture to survive with minor improvements and produced a hardening of the traditional pattern of cultivation and, at the same time, a great growth in population. "Wet-rice cultivation, with its extraordinary ability to maintain levels of marginal labour productivity by always managing to work one more man in without a serious fall in per capita income, soaked up almost the whole of the additional population that Western intrusion created, at least indirectly." [38] To quote another of Geertz's expressive phrases, increasing numbers were "forced into a more and more labour-stuffed sawah pattern," [39] In these circumstances there occurred the over-elaboration of the system which he terms "involution"—the pushing of terraces higher up the slopes of hills, the further fragmentation of land, the practice of double cropping whereby rice is followed during the dry season by corn or legumes, and even the planting of the terrace walls with appropriate crops. Geertz draws

---

[37] Geertz, *The Development of the Javanese Economy*, p. 29. The argument of this working paper was later elaborated more fully in the same author's *Agricultural Involution: The Processes of Ecological Change in Indonesia* (Berkeley and Los Angeles, 1963).

[38] Geertz, *Agricultural Involution*, p. 80.

[39] *Ibid.*

attention to an architectural parallel as a style moves from its classic purity into a stage of overdecoration and decadence. Once the basic forms are fixed and there is no further possibility of structural innovation within that style, its exponents proceed merely to fill in the details, to ornament and refine. So it was in Javanese agriculture. The earliest wet rice stage, he says, was merely "a preliminary sketch," and the time of the Hindu and Moslem states (and also of the Company, when the Dutch impact was still relatively light) saw a filling in of solid detail. The Culture System, however, "brought an overornamentation, a Gothic elaboration of technical and organizational detail," [40] and this was to be carried further under the corporate plantation system.

The effect of agriculture's involution was to accentuate the division, in Indonesia's case, between the advanced and the traditional sectors of her economy, and Geertz's analysis does something to reinstate Boeke's dual economy concept, though in a rigorously modified form. Nor was it merely an economic dualism. The economic dualism was accompanied by a social dichotomy. To go a few miles from Djakarta, Surabaja, or any other major city is to bring oneself into a different world—the world of the village economy and the village society—and environment which, for all of the exceptions which might be quoted, does seem particularly impervious to change. Boeke's analysis performed a service in drawing attention to this. His error was to make the term "dualism" bear too much; loosely used it does embody a good deal of the feel of the divided society which came into being after 1870.

"Plural Society"

The introduction of a highly developed capitalist economy in Indonesia was accompanied by the accentuation of social divisions within the community, and to a considerable extent during the colonial period this division followed racial lines. Europeans governed the colony and virtually controlled the modern economy that their capital had created, Chinese emerged to a dominant position in the retail trade of the islands, and indigenous people, with important exceptions, were confined to the role of peasant cultivators. This sort of broad division of function supplied the basis for a different characterization of the Indonesian scene—that of J. S. Furnivall who developed the

[40] *Ibid.* p. 82.

theme of the plural society. Furnivall, it should be noticed, rejected the main premises of Boeke, though in some ways his own work carried strong echoes of the dualistic theory. He considered that Boeke had underestimated the "economic" propensities of Indonesians and had overstressed the sharpness of the division between capitalism and "precapitalism." [41] He proceeded to argue that, insofar as a duality existed, it was an artificially imposed, rather than a natural, duality. Chinese industry and European dominance between them had stifled the economic development of the Indonesian. Indonesia's backwardness in this view was a direct reflection of the plural character of society.

A plural society by definition was a society "comprising two or more elements or social orders which live side by side, yet without mingling, in one political unit." [42] Plurality of this kind, argued Furnivall, was typical of tropical dependencies, though it was by no means confined to that type of situation. In South Africa, in the United States of America, and in Canada, elements of plurality were to be found. In some cases this plurality was based on color as well as on cultural differences, as in South Africa or the United States. In the Canadian case the different communities were divided by language and religion though both elements were drawn originally from the same Western European cultural tradition. In the case of Ireland the difference was one of religion only. Plurality was thus very much a matter of degree. In tropical countries, however, since rulers and ruled differed in race and color, the degree of plurality was bound to be high. Netherlands India in Furnivall's eyes was a particularly extreme case with her communities sharply divided according to race, color, culture, and economic function.

The central feature of the plural system was the lack of a common will, of a common social demand. Such a society represented almost a federation of allied provinces rather than a state. The only real meeting place for the disparate elements was in the market place.[43] To Furnivall it was this division between separate communities rather than a possible distinction between the capitalist and the precapitalist sector of the economy that should be the focus of attention. In the "native" sector of the economy he saw, indeed, a new emphasis on economic values, admittedly less marked than in other sectors, but

---

[41] *Netherlands India*, pp. 453ff.
[42] *Ibid.*, p. 446.
[43] *Ibid.*, p. 449.

nonetheless present.[44] In the context of a plural society, however, these views were not able to contribute to the growth of a common social demand.

The creation of a new social integration was seen as a political problem, and Furnivall's discussion of the question is reminiscent of the assumptions underlying the Ethical Policy. In normal conditions, he said, quoting De Kat Angelino, society is the parent of the state "whereas in Netherlands India the pressing burden on the State is the creation of Society." [45] He held out no great hope that the task could be easily accomplished, or that ultimate anarchy could be avoided. Furnivall's diagnosis was based upon a study of an apparently stable and secure colonial regime. The conclusion of his argument— that social integration was the only alternative to anarchy—was no doubt sound enough. If the Dutch were to remain as a permanent part of the Indonesian scene it could only be on the basis of De Kat Angelino's East Indian society in some form or other. In the event, time was not to allow the experiment any opportunity of success. If we may look ahead at this point to the post-revolutionary situation, the plural society analysis is now far less relevant than it appeared in the 1930s. Independence has removed the dominant European minority from the racial mosaic, and the other principal minority— the Chinese—is so outnumbered that, in spite of its significant economic power, it is not in a position to challenge Indonesian political supremacy. The plural character of society is far less important in Indonesia's case than it is in the case of Malaysia, for example, where Malay and Chinese are numerically more evenly balanced, or in South Africa, where the white minority holds the reigns of power, or even in the United States, where the Negro, who cannot secede from American society, has nonetheless been, to an important degree, segregated within it. The Chinese do present an important minority problem in modern Indonesia but the dimensions of the problem are hardly such as to make it a central characteristic of contemporary society. In the new situation other divisions have become more important. Rivalry between leading ethnic groups within the Indonesian community has asserted itself as an important obstacle to national unity. The narrowness of the modern elite and the broad gulf separating it from the mass of the agricultural population poses problems of political control. Within the elite itself, divisions between different interest

[44] *Ibid.*, pp. 453 and 457.
[45] *Ibid.*, p. 463.

and skill groups—administrators, political leaders, commercial interests, professional groups such as those trained for military service—create special difficulties of cooperation. Not all of these divisions were apparent during the colonial period; at that time their significance was disguised by the overwhelming facts of Dutch political control and economic dominance. In the context of today, they appear much more important than differences of race or culture, and they have rightly captured the attention of later analysts of the Indonesian scene.

Divisions within the Elite

The role played by the class of Western-educated leaders produced by the educational policies of the Ethical Period was out of all proportion to its size. In fact those policies touched only a handful, comparatively speaking, of the country's 60 or 65 million people. In 1940 88,223 Indonesians were enrolled in schools giving a Western primary education.[46] The 6 per cent literacy rate at the close of the 1930s has already been mentioned, and but a tiny fraction had secured a tertiary or even a secondary education. An indication of how few these were may be gathered from the fact that in 1940 only 240 Indonesians graduated from high schools.[47] These figures suggest in striking fashion the smallness of Indonesia's modern leadership, and, in some degree, justify the image of her society as comprising a peasant mass surmounted by a minute elite.

It is somewhat objectionable, morally and sociologically, no doubt to speak in terms of the "mass" of the population: the mass is comprised of individuals and may also be classified in terms of innumerable groups. The purpose of using the term in this context is simply to sharpen the contrast between a tradition-oriented peasantry making up most of the population and an urban political leadership dominated by persons of high Western education, to draw attention to the smallness of the latter group, and to stress the absence of intermediate classes. Indonesia, in brief, by the end of the Dutch rule was a society without a middle class. Certainly there was no strong indigenous commercial element to bridge the gap between the elite and the population in general. It has been seen that, from the beginning of the East India Company's operations, Dutch policy had aimed at commercial monopoly and in time this had stifled the expansion

[46] Kahin, op. cit., p. 31.
[47] Ibid.

of indigenous commerce. This was, of course, a matter of degree. There were areas where local and even wider trading operations remained in indigenous hands. In West Sumatra and in North and South Celebes, for example, there continued to exist a strong tradition of commercial activity. Even in Java itself, despite the more prolonged Dutch control of the island as a whole, a small trading and industrial element survived, the latter confined mainly to the batik industry and to the production of the scented kretek cigarette. But Dutch policy, Chinese competition and, in the twentieth century, the import of Western manufactured textile and other goods prevented the proper development of this class. As Kahin concluded: "If one can speak of an Indonesian middle class, its entrepreneurial element had been almost eliminated by the circumstances attending three centuries of Dutch rule." [48] Kahin does use the term middle class, but applies it to the emergent elite itself—the small class of persons with some degree of Western education who had obtained employment as clerks and officials. Of this class it could be said that it "was not only predominantly noncapitalistic, but that for the most part it consisted of salaried employees, most of whom were civil servants." [49] The important fact about it was that it did not form a broad, numerous, and mediating bourgeoisie which by its very existence could blur the edges of class divisions in a hierarchical social order. One's attention is caught rather by the sharpness of the division by which this class itself was separated, even in colonial times, from the population of Indonesia in general.

The term "elite," of course, still presents some problems of definition and classification. Different observers clearly have had different tests in mind when they used the term. Some have spoken of a mere 200 to 500 persons,[50] and others of 1,000.[51] Either of these figures would imply a limitation of the term to those actually in positions of power, with the consequence that membership of the elite might change from time to time as individuals rose or fell from influence and power. The one person might be a member of the elite at one time and not at another. Others have used the term in a broad sense

[48] *Ibid.*, p. 29.
[49] *Ibid.*
[50] Herbert Feith, *The Decline of Constitutional Democracy in Indonesia* (Ithaca, New York, 1962), pp. 108ff.
[51] George McT. Kahin, "Indonesia" in Kahin, ed., *Major Governments of Asia* (Ithaca, New York, 1958), p. 526.

to suggest the groups from which the actual holders of power have been drawn.[52] Feith, in dealing with the Indonesian Republic, has used an image of concentric circles in his analysis of political awareness and participation. The inner circle—the "political elite"—is extremely small, consisting of between 200 and 500 persons all of whom are "steeped in the all-Indonesian urban culture that had grown up around the nationalist movement." [53] The next circle contains the "political public"—people outside the elite "who saw themselves as capable of taking action that could affect national government or politics." [54] This group, which shared, in some measure, in the modern, urban-centered culture of the elite, and whose membership, he suggests, was perhaps indicated most clearly by the test of regular newspaper reading, might be between a million and one-and-a-half million. Finally the outermost circle contains the mass. The question at issue is really whether one's model is best constructed in simple terms of "elite" versus "mass" or whether the elite itself is to be divided into two parts, the actual wielders of influence at any time and the larger, but still comparatively tiny, body of the articulate and politically aware. Even a million is a small enough group in a population of 100 million. In the present chapter the term "elite" is used in a less restricted sense than that of Feith, but it is not intended to take in more than a fraction of the larger "political public."

In spite of the smallness—by any test—of this group, it was far from being homogeneous. Important distinctions could be observed within it. There was first of all a distinction, which will have already become apparent, between the old *priyayi*—those who belonged by birth to an older aristocracy and whose function as local rulers on behalf of a higher authority had been carefully safeguarded and even extended by the Dutch—and the newer official class of which we have been speaking—a class that had been produced by Western education and employed in the expanded civil service of the later years of Dutch rule. Some of the latter were drawn from families of the lesser aristocracy but others were commoners. The distinction has become increasingly less important. Even though the employment of

---

[52] See, *e.g.*, Guy J. Pauker, "The role of political organizations in Indonesia," *Far Eastern Survey*, Vol. 27, No. 9 (September 1958).

[53] Feith, *op. cit.*, p. 109.

[54] *Ibid.*, p. 108.

Indonesian officials was confined almost exclusively to subordinate positions, government service still carried with it a certain status which, in time, was to blur the distinction between old and new *priyayi* and to undermine the older status system based on birth.

Again a distinction may be made between those who accepted such employment in government service and those who, instead, were drawn into political action within the framework of the growing nationalist movement. This division has been described by one observer in terms of a contrast between a "functional" and a "political" elite.[55] The distinction cuts across that between older *priyayi* and new men. The functional elite included those who saw their duty as being to keep things going—to keep the wheels of government turning smoothly whatever their long-range political hopes and political sympathies. The political elite were concerned in varying degrees with political organization and direct action in resistance to Dutch authority. They were not necessarily all concerned with violent revolution, and many were willing to envisage a path to independence through cooperation with the Dutch. But in broad terms their aim was to disturb the status quo. The functional elite may have looked ultimately to nationalist success also, but their immediate obligation was to keep the status quo in working order and perhaps to play their part in securing an increasing absorption of Indonesian elements into the service of government. The attainment of limited and practical reforms within the framework of the colonial system represented their main political aim. "These men were not inclined to take idealistic excursions; they were practical administrators." [56] These two approaches did not necessarily correspond to differences of social origin. The ranks of the political elite contained *priyayi* as well as "new men." And though the functional elite included older members of the territorial service who were traditional, or as van Niel puts it, "cosmologically oriented," in outlook, it was composed more typically of those who were modern and "welfare-state oriented" in outlook[57]— men whose status depended upon education and office rather than on birth. From the older *priyayi*, however, came standards of behavior and service that set a pattern to be emulated by many of

---

[55] The distinction forms a central theme in Robert van Niel, *The Emergence of the Modern Indonesian Elite* (The Hague and Bandung, 1960).

[56] *Ibid.*, p. 242.

[57] *Ibid.*, p. 2.

the new and younger public servants. "They set the example of devotion to duty that came to characterize most Indonesian civil servants, and they placed this devotion above any particular group or ideology which controlled the political institutions of the country. Here . . . came to be found those persons who held Indonesian society together and kept it functioning in its modern fashion." [58]

Whether functional elite or political elite, whether older aristocracy or new men, the emphasis so far in these paragraphs has been placed very much on the importance of Western education, and with good reason, for this was the single most important formative factor in determining the character of the elite. Surveys made of political leadership during the early years of the independent republic of Indonesia revealed the fact that the overwhelming majority of these leaders had had a Western education in some form. One estimate based upon a study of cabinet ministers, members of parliament, and senior civil servants of the early republic, revealed that the overwhelming majority of these—91 per cent of the members of parliament, 94 per cent of the ministers, and 100 per cent of the civil servants—had received a Western type of education at senior high school or tertiary level.[59] This was, of course, a particularly narrow group. If one were to apply the term "elite" a little more widely than that, the role of Western education would still prove to be an important element, but it would be necessary to take rather more account of Moslem education also, especially in the modernist tradition to which reference was made in an earlier chapter. The educational role of Muhammadiyah, for example, was of great importance for those who wished to achieve some sort of reconcilitaion between Islam and Western thought; and reformist Islamic thought was important as a constituent in the outlook even of many Western-educated leaders of Indonesian nationalism.

Finally, underlying other distinctions and divisions there was to be observed a broad difference in outlook that may be defined partly in ethnic terms, partly in terms of political tradition, partly in terms of religious feeling, and partly in terms of social and economic ethos. This was the division which Herbert Feith has described in terms

[58] *Ibid.,* p. 165.
[59] Soelaeman Soemardi, "Some Aspects of the Social Origin of the Indonesian Political Decision-Makers" (Transactions of the Third World Congress of Sociology, London, 1956).

of two principal "political-cultures" within Indonesian society—
"Javanese-aristocratic" and "Islamic-entrepreneurial." [60] The ethnic
element was perhaps the least important aspect of this contrast.
Education, the extension of Dutch rule, and the expansion of the
new economy had cut across the lines of ethnic division and had
helped to forge a new nationalist unity at least as far as the elite
was concerned. Even so, ethnic self-consciousness was not wholly
removed, and, in particular, the broad opposition between the
Javanese as the largest single group, and all other groups, was a
continuing factor of some significance. More important, however,
in explaining the character of the two cultures were certain historical
factors. One of these was the uneven penetration of Islam into the
archipelago—the slightness of its impact in east and central Java as
compared with its strength in coastal commercial centers and their
hinterlands, especially in Sumatra and south Celebes and Borneo. A
second was the uneven impact of Dutch rule, which, with the exception of a handful of trading centers, made itself effective outside
Java only towards the end of the nineteenth century. Third, there
were also present the differences deriving from an earlier tradition
still—differences between the inland agricultural bureaucratic society
of Java and the less rigid, more enterprising maritime states that drew
their strength from trade. These factors combined to produce a contrast in outlook which is sufficiently marked to justify Feith's distinction between two political cultures. The Javanese-aristocratic culture
was "contemptuous of economic pursuits" while the Islamic-entrepreneurial was respectful. The Javanese-aristocratic culture looked to
the formation of a secular state, was more anti-Dutch, was more
nativistic, had a greater inclination towards socialist ideas. The
Islamic-entrepreneurial culture desired an Islamic state, but was in
general more sympathetic to ideas stemming from the West. It was
also a little more individualist and less collectivist in outlook.

This contrast can only be drawn in broad terms. As Feith points
out, it was far from covering all cases, and there were many individuals who combined features of both outlooks. It is an important
contrast, nevertheless. We have already noticed its presence as a
continuing theme in Indonesian history over more than a thousand
years. In a new form it was to be of fundamental importance during
the early years of independence when it conditioned conflicting views
of the nature of the state and of its tasks.

[60] Feith, *op. cit.*, pp. 30-32.

If Dutch imperialism in the late nineteenth and early twentieth centuries is to be regarded as representing a new cultural challenge to a traditional order—or to a complex of traditional orders—in the Indies, its success was far from complete by the eve of World War II. Certainly it had set in motion changes that, in character and scope, were markedly different from those to be observed in the two-and-a-half centuries before 1870. It had not achieved more than the beginnings of "westernization," but, by chance as well as by deliberation, it had set in motion forces of "modernization," which is not quite the same thing. Its economic impact had helped to disrupt the comparatively stable patterns of indigenous societies and had begun to awaken mass discontents. At the same time it stimulated the growth of a new leadership—narrowly based and in some ways reflecting traditional attitudes as well as new ones.

SIX

NATIONALISM

The emergence of a nationalist movement in the first decades of the twentieth century was essentially a new phenomenon. There had been movements of resistance against the Dutch from time to time in the past—the Java War of 1825 or the struggle in West Sumatra in the 1820s and 1830s for example—and these, in retrospect, might seem to have been the forerunners of a later, more coherent, resistance to colonial rule. Indeed they have been so regarded by modern nationalists themselves, and the leaders of the early revolts have become heroes of the modern republic. More correctly, however, these were prenationalist movements, isolated, uncoordinated responses to particular discontents, sporadic in character and reflective of fissures within Indonesian society as well as hostility to the spread of Dutch power.[1] The same sort of comment could be made about the Atjeh Wars at the end of the century, which opposed the imposition of Dutch authority at the northern tip of Sumatra. Nationalism by contrast represented a positive movement—the operation of a new ideological force concerned not merely with resistance to Dutch domination but with the forging of a new national entity.

In this respect, the Indonesian experience may be seen as part of

[1] Cf. G. McT. Kahin, *Nationalism and Revolution in Indonesia*, pp. 41-42. Kahin argues that embryonic nationalisms existed within Indonesian societies from the period of the first Dutch impact. But Kahin's own treatment goes on to stress the different character of organized twentieth-century nationalism.

a broader movement to be observed elsewhere in Asia. It was paralleled, for instance, by the growth of a coherent nationalism in India. Just as the Padri Wars had little to do with the rise of Indonesian nationalism so the emergence of a nationalist movement in India represented a different order of activity from that expressed in the Indian mutiny. Even in countries such as China, which was not a colonial dependency, there could be observed in the twentieth century the attempt to fashion new ideological foundations for the state. It was no accident that the first of Sun Yat-sen's three principles, intended to provide a platform for the Kuomintang, was the principle of nationalism. Sun's objective was in part to mobilize resistance to the dominant economic position enjoyed in China by the Western powers (this was, perhaps, a counterpart to the idea of resistance to colonial rule in Indonesia or India) but it went far beyond that. The Chinese empire was a society rather than a modern state and Sun's aim was to create a new political order which could command the prior loyalty of its subjects over such traditional points of loyalty as the family. In the case of Indonesia, too, the struggle for political independence and the attempt to develop a united national sentiment, able to knit together the distinct societies of the archipelago and to lay the foundations of a modern Indonesian state, were two sides of the same coin.

The development of an organized nationalist movement was a product of Dutch imperialism in its later stages. Its comparative lateness may seem at first glance surprising. Though the propagandist picture of 350 years of Dutch rule in the Indies was, as we have seen, a grossly exaggerated one, it was nonetheless true that the island of Java had been subjected to continuous Dutch contact from the seventeenth century and to a fairly profound degree of control from the mid-eighteenth century. In the nineteenth century, moreover, Holland had engaged in a degree of systematic exploitation of the island that might have been expected to evoke violent opposition. It was not merely length of contact that was important, it would seem, nor was it entirely the harshness of Dutch policy that led to the rise of organized nationalism. On the contrary the formation of activist societies dedicated to the struggle for independence coincided with attempts on the part of the Netherlands to remedy past wrongs and to earn for herself a reputation for enlightened colonial rule.

The Dutch prided themselves on their performance as colonial overlords. Certainly if one were to try to draw up a moral balance sheet of their imperialism, its credit side would compare very favorably with that of other European colonial powers. Attention has already been drawn to the fact that, even in the heyday of laissez-faire, certain protective limitations were imposed on the entry of Dutch capital. The Agrarian Law and the Coolie Ordinance represented, by the standards of the day, an enlightened attempt to safeguard Indonesian land and to protect the bargaining position of the laborer as he entered European employment. More positively the ideals that inspired the Ethical Policy represented a concept of colonial responsibility that set a pattern for other colonial powers to follow. But the consequences of that idealism were sometimes disconcerting. The very efficiency that Holland brought to bear in the execution of the Ethical Policy (and efficiency in the highest degree was a hallmark of Dutch government in the Indies) was productive of resentment. Indonesian villagers, compelled by gentle pressure to improve roads, or to extend irrigation works or to perform other tasks which their colonial masters held to be for their own good, were far from appreciative, and came to dislike the degree of close supervision that paternal rule imposed. There was a jibe quoted by Furnivall that "the villager cannot even scratch his head, unless an expert shows him how to do it and the sub-district officer gives him permission." [2] And at a higher level the educational policies of the Indies government helped to produce the very class of frustrated persons that could give nationalist feeling articulate leadership. This is not an uncommon experience in the annals of colonial rule. Colonial welfare policies tend to produce the reverse of gratitude—only the colonial power itself would expect otherwise—and it might not seem too much to say that, in Indonesia's case, its nationalist movement was the product of the virtues rather than the vices of Dutch rule.

On the debit side there were some entries to be made nonetheless. There were the usual discriminations, some petty, some substantial, which are inevitable in any colonial situation. Holland imposed no formal color bar in the Indies. Indonesians of appropriate rank or education were not rigidly excluded from Dutch society. Society was also prepared to accept, and the regime to favor, persons of mixed

[2] J. S. Furnivall, *Netherlands India*, p. 389.

parentage.[3] But a social color bar existed to a considerable degree in practice. The increase in the Dutch population after 1870, and the change in its character as wives accompanied their husbands and began to create a new and self-sufficient pattern of expatriate society, led to the erection of barriers of social intercourse across racial frontiers.[4] The psychological consequences of this exclusion of educated Indonesians from Dutch society were incalculable. Economically the educated Indonesian found himself subject to discrimination in favor of the Dutch in his search for employment commensurate with his skill. There were measures, also, designed to protect the interests of Dutch enterprise against the competition of native enterprise—as in the different prices paid to European and Indonesian rubber producers[5] or the more favorable quota allowed to estate rubber during the rubber restriction schemes of the 1920s and 1930s.

In more general terms, and apart from such instances as these, the genuine altruism of the Ethical Policy could not entirely disguise the essential self-interest of Dutch policy. Benevolence is a matter of degree, and Holland was more rather than less benevolent. But still her primary purpose in being in the Indies at all was a commercial, not a benevolent one—imperial powers after all do not hold colonies for the purpose of pursuing welfare programs in them—and the pressure of investing interests demanded the pursuit of policies that would assist them to make profits. The welfare side of policy was possible only insofar as it did not conflict except in a marginal way with the primary economic goal. This limitation was not apparent to van Deventer and the followers of his idea, for they did not see any fundamental inconsistency between European investment and Indonesian welfare. Basically they still accepted the liberal

[3] The position of the Eurasian community was to prove an irritant to the Indonesian nationalist and was to evoke its own reaction after independence. For one discussion of the problem, see Paul W. van der Veur, "The Eurasians of Indonesia: Castaways of Colonialism," *Pacific Affairs*, XXVII (1954).

[4] The influence of women on colonial policy is a subject that merits more attention. An unmarried man pioneering the frontiers of empire easily reaches an accommodation with the society he finds there. It may sometimes be a sexual accommodation but a mistress can also be a bridge to understanding. But when a man arrives with a wife and children, a slice of his homeland is added that inevitably affects his adaptability and binds him by chains of respectability to whatever conventions might be the current ones at home.

[5] Kahin, *op. cit.*, p. 56.

assumption that the increased development resulting from the application of European capital would, in the long run, benefit the indigenous inhabitants as well as the Dutch. The Ethical Policy must accordingly be regarded as merely a minor modification of the liberal policy.

In the end, however, this attempt to draw up a balance sheet—to set virtues against vices—is not very helpful; or at least the differences with which it is concerned are marginal differences when seen in the light of the total picture. Dutch rule in the Indies was not particularly harsh, but this fact is not closely relevant to a consideration of the roots of nationalism. Nationalism, in fact, was not the product of oppressive rule but of deeper forces of social change that accompanied the new economic development and that could neither be checked by the protective aspects of Dutch policy nor channelled into desired directions by positive welfare programs. The disruption of the social patterns of the village and the undermining of many of its customary certainties aroused broad dissatisfaction, and produced also a new awareness of the outside world. The presence of government was felt, of course, more sharply, and there was a new knowledge too of the vast economic order lying beyond the horizon of the village but reacting upon it. The profound psychological effects of this dislocation of tradition were laid bare, to cite one example, in West Sumatra when a committee was appointed to investigate the causes of the Communist revolt of 1926. Its report referred to the individualizing effects following the penetration of a new economy: the pledging of land, the slackening of family ties, the weakening of the authority of *adat* leaders of the community, all of which combined to provide a ready environment for the growth of mass movements of resistance to Dutch authority.[6] At the same time the growing cities were the cradle of a new culture, detached in great measure from tradition, and able to transcend loyalties to particular ethnic groups. Within this modern urban culture, the rise of the Western-educated elite provided leadership that could help to crystallize mass discontents and to formulate a new vision of an Indonesian nation.

The understanding of these processes can be aided by the attempts

---

[6] The report was prepared by B. J. O. Schrieke on behalf of the committee, and part of it is published in Schrieke, *Indonesian Sociological Studies*, I (The Hague, 1955), p. 85.

of some scholars to come to grips with the phenomenon of national-ism in a broader setting, and especially with the variant of national-ism to be observed in underdeveloped countries in general. While Asian and African nationalism in the twentieth century has strong ideological ties with European nationalist thinking,[7] it has clearly differed greatly from those nineteenth-century movements toward national integration in western Europe, where ties of common language, territorial contiguity, the existence of a common stock of traditions and a common history, and the growth of economic rela-tions have contributed to the formation of larger and more powerful political units. Even in Europe the task of identifying the common ingredients making for the rise of a nation is difficult. Linguistic unity would not seem to be necessary. Switzerland has welded the speakers of two languages into one people making each group closer to the other than either is to the speakers of its own language in neighboring France or Germany. A common territory and a common history cannot insure a common outlook. Different peoples within one politi-cal unit may remain deeply divided from each other, as was the case with Germans and Czechs in Czechoslovakia. And as Karl Deutsch says, the idea of a common territory seems to beg the ques-tion. "In what sense is there a territorial community or contiguity between a German village on the Swiss border and a German village on the shores of the North Sea? In what sense does this contiguity differ from that with a Swiss village five miles across the political border?" [8] The Jews, as he points out, possessed a sense of national identity for centuries while possessing no common territory at all. In underdeveloped areas nationalism has often been concerned to unite groups separated by language and ethnic differences within political boundaries that have been quite arbitrarily defined by the accidents of colonial rule. To that extent it has sought to create artificial units when the "natural" bases of unity might well seem to be tenuous.

In these areas the roots of nationalism may be found in new economic pressures that have disrupted the traditional social order, stimulated the emergence of new classes and contributed to the modernization of the society concerned. One attempt to abstract the

[7] See Elie Kedourie, *Nationalism* (London, 1960) for a consideration of Euro-pean nationalism as an ideological strand in French revolutionary doctrine and in later political thought.

[8] Karl W. Deutsch, *Nationalism and Social Communication: An Enquiry into the Foundations of Nationality* (New York, 1953).

essential elements in this type of situation is that of John H. Kautsky,[9] whose analysis rests on his identification of a common pattern of traditional classes in such societies—a narrow aristocracy, an ignorant and isolated peasantry, and a middle class of craftsmen and tradesmen—and a common pattern of new classes—a late-developing nascent capitalist class, an industrial working class (with which may be included plantation laborers as well as urban workers), and a professional class of white collar workers and intellectuals. It is the latter who became the vanguard of the drive for modernization and the essential element in the development of nationalism. They are able to find support for their movement both among the traditional orders of society and among the newly emerging classes of capitalists and workers. The peasantry may be largely indifferent to the wider goals of nationalism but the effects of the colonial economic revolution are felt even within the village, and as the peasant meets the pressure of these new impersonal forces he comes to provide raw material for a mass movement which he cannot direct and does not properly understand. The indigenous middle class suffers more directly from the establishment of the new economy and is obviously resentful of its colonial character. The aristocracy is in a more ambiguous position. Colonial governments often found it convenient to rule through this class (as the Dutch, for example, made administrative use of the Javanese *priyayi*) and therefore protected it and bound it to some extent to the colonial regime. In this sense "colonialism is thus not only a modernizing influence, but also a conservative force." [10] But in transforming the basis of an agrarian society it also threatens the source of power of traditional aristocracies and may therefore lead them to join in nationalist movements. As far as the new classes are concerned, the anti-colonial grievances of the working class are obvious and the new capitalist class, though in some respects it may be tied to the colonial economy, is nonetheless likely to suffer from the competition of foreign-owned commercial establishments, and to look therefore to the opportunities that independence might bring. But both of these groups are likely to be organizationally weak, leaving the main initiating role to the intel-

[9] John H. Kautsky, "An Essay in the Politics of Development"—an extended introductory essay in Kautsky, ed., *Political Change in Underdeveloped Countries: Nationalism and Communism* (New York, 1963).
[10] *Ibid.*, p. 42.

lectuals—men who have been trained by the colonial power and who have absorbed some of the ideas and values of Western civilization. They have become, to some extent, displaced persons in their own society but have not been adequately employed by the colonial regime. Colonialism "produces the intellectuals and yet by its very existence it frustrates them."[11] This class above all is anxious to modernize colonial society and to seek its political rewards in so doing.[12]

Other observers, too, have stressed in different ways the initiating role of the intellectual. As Harry Benda puts it, the occupational structure of advanced societies is such as to make the intelligentsia adjuncts to other social classes rather than a class in their own right, whereas in non-Western societies they come to wield political power "as it were independently, i.e., they wield it in their own right, as intelligentsias, rather than as spokesmen for entrenched social forces."[13] In seeking this authority, according to Shils, they are seeking in part a new authority to which to submit to replace that with which they have broken.[14] The "authoritative collectivity" they seek is the "nation" and more particularly the organized movement for national independence.[15] (Of importance too, however, is his point that intellectuals are less "cut off" from their own culture than some observers assert and than they themselves sometimes feel. They are, however, the subjects of a tension between two cultures, which may sometimes show itself in a nativistic reaction that leads them to extol the virtues of traditional culture.)

These broader analyses have obvious relevance for the Indonesian

[11] Ibid., p. 49.

[12] A part of Kautsky's argument, into which it is not necessary to enter here, is his view that in underdeveloped areas Communism has tended to draw its strength from the same roots as has nationalism, and has become more and more identical with nationalism. See a critique of this argument by Richard Lowenthal—"Communism and Nationalism" in Problems of Communism, Vol. XI, No. 6 (November-December 1962).

[13] Harry J. Benda, "Non-Western Intelligentsias as Political Elites," in Kautsky, ed., op. cit., p. 237.

[14] Edward A. Shils, "The Intellectuals in the Political Development of the New States," in Kautsky, ed., op. cit., p. 207. Of relevance also is his The Intellectual Between Tradition and Modernity: The Indian Situation (Comparative Studies in Society and History, Supplement 1, The Hague, 1961).

[15] Shils refers to the "party of national independence" rather than the "movement," but in Indonesia, as will be seen, the movement was not united in a single party. The general point, however, may still apply.

case.[16] There the Western-educated intellectual elite was able to take an initiative in nationalist organization, and in so doing it could canalize mass frustrations and resentments arising from the profound disturbance which colonization had brought to the settled patterns of agrarian life. These developments were more important even than the welding of the archipelago into one clear economic and political unit, though this was important too. Notwithstanding the past glories of Srivijaya and Madjapahit, the political entity created by the Dutch, with its more tightly constructed governmental organization, was very different from the kind of suzerainty which Madjapahit may (or may not) have exercised. The important thing, however, was not so much the tighter geographical unity as the emergence of a nationalist leadership that could take Madjapahit as a symbol and could appeal to history to underwrite the idea of national identity.

Goals of Nationalism

The vision of an Indonesian nation was perceived only in general terms. There was room for differences in the way it might be envisaged in detail and room also for differences of opinion about the method of realizing it. Such a small elite leadership might well have been expected to achieve uniformity of outlook; in fact nationalism displayed considerable variety whether one thinks in terms of political philosophy or in terms of organization.

Certainly the common background of Western education did represent a powerful unifying factor in the fashioning of a national-

[16] At a more abstract level the conceptual analysis of Karl Deutsch in his *Nationalism and Social Communication* (New York, 1953) offers important suggestions for the further investigation of nationalism in Asia. Deutsch rejects attempts to define the phenomenon of nationalism in terms primarily of common language or territory or history or culture, though he recognizes that any or all of these ingredients may be relevant. He invokes the aid of a series of social disciplines and proceeds to develop the concept of "uneven cluster distributions" of settlement, transport, centers of culture, centers of language, class divisions, barriers between markets, regional differences in wealth, and interdependence. All of these "act together to produce a highly differentiated and clustered world of regions, peoples, and nations" within which it is possible to test empirically the density or scarcity of resulting social communications (p. 161). His conclusion is that "the community which permits a common history to be experienced as common, is a community of complementary habits and facilities of communication" (p. 70) and that these can be mapped. The concept of social communications as being the essential element in the making of a "people" may be relevant for Indonesia where a variety of differences—ethnic, linguistic, social, economic— have been bridged in marked degree by common sentiment after the establishment of a new economy, of a coherent communications system, of a common language.

ist outlook. The Indonesian intellectual was brought into touch with existing currents of European liberal and radical thought, which fed his nationalism and gave to his political philosophy a secular, democratic, and socialist flavor. Liberal views of the state and of the nature of political authority provided a justification for resistance to a government that was not merely authoritarian but was alien into the bargain. The study of Dutch history, too, played its part, as Kahin points out, in fostering ideals of resistance to foreign rule; for the Indonesian nationalist the rise of the Dutch republic and its struggle against foreign oppression offered plenty of parallels that could be applied to his own situation.[17] And the ready acceptance of some of the main themes of Western thought was accompanied in the case of many Indonesian nationalists by an almost self-conscious rejection of the local tradition—a fact that was to create problems for the Indonesian intellectual after independence.

A more radical ingredient was provided by Marxist thought, whose general analysis of the nature of Western imperialism carried an appeal extending well beyond the ranks of the Social Democratic Association, which in 1921 became the Indonesian Communist Party. For those outside the Party, Marxism as a system did not necessarily conflict with the general nationalist commitment to democratic institutions, but it injected an element of toughness and rigor into what might otherwise have been a utopian body of political ideas. It provided a recognition of the role of force in human affairs, a conviction that the Dutch would prove unable to make concessions that would inevitably conflict with their clear economic interest, and a consequent awareness of the need for struggle. These elements underlay the noncooperative sectors of organized nationalism.

Western ideas were not confined solely to the secular sections of the movement. Many of the intellectual values that were derived from Western sources had their impact even within the framework of Islamic education. This was in part an unexpected consequence of the Netherlands' own educational policy in the Indies. Toward the end of the nineteenth century, Dutch fears of the pan-Islamic movement, popular among pilgrims returning from Mecca, had led to a reconsideration by the Indies government of its Islamic policy. The government's adviser on Islamic matters, Christiaan Snouck Hurgronje, however, played down the dangers of such a movement, pointing out that Islam was not a united and ecclesiastically organized

[17] Kahin, *op. cit.*, p. 49.

faith, that it was not necessarily fanatical, and that in Indonesia it had been forced to compromise with custom. On the other hand Snouck did consider that the individual Moslem fanatic might be a potential danger, and he counseled religious tolerance combined with vigilance against political movements based on Islam. More significantly he looked to Western education to free Indonesians from subservience to *adat* and Islam alike and to make possible the emergence of a new society.[18] Snouck's view was influential and was one of the reasons for the extension of general educational facilities after 1900. In fact the plan did not produce the desired aim. Western education played its part in strengthening the modernistic strain within Indonesian Islam, which, as we have seen, was concerned to strip from Islam the accretions which had come to obscure the purity of its doctrine, and to seek some kind of adjustment between the faith itself and modern thought. The modernist movement in the end was to become a distinct and major threat to the colonial regime, for it was through modernism that Islam was able to contribute to, and to share in, nationalist thought and organization. Modernist Islam offered one of the more radical challenges to Dutch rule in the early days of the movement through the leadership of the mass organization Sarekat Islam (though it would be misleading to describe the society itself as representing a modernist approach).

Despite large areas of common accord, however, there did remain important differences of outlook, both between Islamic nationalists and secular nationalists, and within the ranks of the secular nationalists themselves. Islamic nationalists looked ultimately to the establishment of an Islamic state, and they recognized, and were naturally suspicious of, the agnostic character of liberal thought. Such suspicions led eventually to a growing split within the broad body of nationalist feeling.[19] Secular nationalism as a separate organized force eventually emerged in the late 1920s. Secondly the rise of the Indonesian Communist Party in the 1920s evoked a major division in nationalist ranks as to means and ultimate goals.[20] Despite the

[18] Harry J. Benda, "Christiaan Snouck Hurgronje and the Foundations of Dutch Islamic Policy in Indonesia," *The Journal of Modern History*, Vol. XXX, 1958.

[19] See Benda, *The Crescent and the Rising Sun*, Chapter II, for an account of the early connection between reformism and radical political organization, and for the later breach between both Muhammadiyah and Sarekat Islam on the one hand, and secular nationalism on the other.

[20] The Indies Social Democratic Association was founded in 1914 as a result of the initiative of Hendrik Sneevliet (formerly of the Netherlands Social Democratic Labor Party, and later, under the name of Maring, the first Comintern

Marxist flavor that pervaded a good deal of the nationalist outlook, the disciplined and purposeful approach of the Communist Party, first in its attempt to seize control of Sarekat Islam from within and then in its independent bid for power in the revolts of 1926 and 1927, constituted a major divisive element within the movement as a whole.

If Communism and Islamic nationalism each had its own distinctive vision of an independent Indonesia, the remaining sectors of the nationalist movement had no very precise political philosophy or clearly conceived program of action. In terms of immediate policy they differed as to the degree to which they were willing to work for the time being within the colonial framework. In terms of general outlook, for all their acceptance of the broad ideals of democratic socialism, they had not worked out in any degree of detail the actual implications of either democratic or socialist theory. There was no very clear discussion, for example, of the practical character of a democratic system—of the problems of securing proper representation, of the nature of party activity, of the methods of controlling an executive, or of the guarantees of individual liberty. General principle stated in general terms was the rule, rather than any precise analysis of the problems of building and operating a democratic state.[21]

The emptiness of a good deal of nationalist political thinking was, perhaps, hardly surprising in view of the lack of opportunity for Indonesian leaders to enjoy practical experience of the processes of government At the regional level after 1903, some provision was made for Indonesian participation in local government, and this experiment was extended in a somewhat more systematic fashion after 1922. Local councils were established in regencies and in muncipalities and later at the provincial level. At the central level the Volksraad, or Peoples Council, which was opened in 1918 was intended to associate local opinion—Indonesian but also Dutch and

---

agent in China). The Social Democratic Association attracted to its ranks certain leading members of the Semarang branch of Sarekat Islam, notably Semaun, who thus became the spearhead of a movement of Marxist infiltration of Sarekat Islam. In 1921 SDA was converted into the Indonesian Communist Party with Semaun as chairman.

[21] *The Birth of Pantjasila* (Djakarta, 1950), quoted at length in Kahin, *op. cit.*, pp. 123-127, gives some indication of the general character of much nationalist thinking as it had developed by the eve of the proclamation of independence. There is as yet little discussion available in English of the detailed character of prewar nationalist thought.

"foreign Asiatic"—with the Indies government. None of these experiments was very thoroughgoing or very successful. The local councils that were formed under the two decentralization experiments were extremely limited in their powers and were kept closely under the control of the central government's territorial administrative service. Officers of that service acted as chairmen of regency and provincial councils and, in practice, the role of the councils was little more than an advisory one to a central official. Their creation did not represent a serious breach in the highly centralized administrative system evolved by the Dutch, and in consequence they did not serve as an effective training ground in political activity. In any case their Indonesian members were drawn almost entirely from the ranks of lower officials, not from political organizations.

The Volksraad was very little better. Like the local councils it provided for representation of the three communities, Dutch, Indonesian, and foreign Asiatic. The Dutch were heavily over-represented, having twenty-five seats in a total Volksraad of sixty. Indonesians had thirty seats and others five.[22] The Indonesian component was made up of twenty elected and ten appointed members, the former being chosen on the basis of a system of indirect election in which local councils were the electoral colleges. The effect was to insure the return of lower government officials rather than the emerging political leaders of the Indonesian community. In any case the very limited powers of the assembly destroyed any prospects it might have offered for experience in the operation of representative institutions, or in the exercise of authority. The governor general could consult the Volksraad on any matter and it had the right of free expression, of petition, and of questioning. After constitutional changes in 1925 its consent was required for the budget, but this seemingly important concession was negated by the provision that, in case of deadlock between government and Volksraad, the budget was to be referred to the States General at The Hague. In consequence, since they were denied any real responsibility, it was not surprising that the Indonesian members of the Assembly should resort to irresponsible criticism of government. Nationalist leaders were divided as to whether they should cooperate by accepting positions in the Volksraad and, in fact, the mainstream of nationalist feeling and nationalist organization did pass it by. Certainly little practical

[22] These proportions were those existing after an increase in membership in 1925.

experience of the character of democracy could be gained from it.[23]

If the ideal of democracy was a vague aspiration rather than a clearly formulated political goal, the same was true of the socialist strand in nationalist thinking. With the exception of the Communist Party, nationalist organizations had not committed themselves to anything approaching a doctrinaire socialism, but had been content with a very general belief in social justice, a suspicion of the power of private capital and a recognition of the fact that representative institutions were not enough in themselves to guarantee a fair distribution of this world's goods. From these there flowed an acceptance of the idea that it was the role of the state to create a just and prosperous society, but no very clear notion of how this was to be done.

The predisposition toward a collectivist approach to economic and social problems was not surprising in view of the character of the nationalist leadership and the circumstances within which the struggle was conducted. Given the fact that the Indonesian elite was predominately an administrative class whose members were employed, insofar as they could find appropriate employment at all, in the lower echelons of the public service or of business administration, it was perhaps natural that they should adopt a bureaucratic rather than an entrepreneurial approach to problems of economic development and social welfare. Apart from other considerations the State appeared to be the only body that could launch a program of development. Even the small commercial class that did exist showed no great attachment to principles of free enterprise as distinct from a socialist order of society. This was due in part to the nature of the Netherlands' economic stake in the Indies. Dutch investment after 1870 had led to the creation, not of a class of small-scale independent planters in Indonesia, but to the growth of the large estate companies and agency houses. The Indonesian businessman thus found his horizon dominated not merely by foreign capital but by corporative enterprises whose headquarters were not even in the Indies but in

---

[23] The Volksraad presents a contrast in principle to the British colonial device of the legislative council. The legislative council was given extensive powers of legislation, but its membership was controlled by the method of nominating unofficial members and by that of preserving an official majority. Responsibility might then be extended by stages, leading ultimately to the election of an unofficial majority. The Volksraad, on the other hand, imposed no official majority and almost from the beginning saw most of its members elected. In these circumstances, however, the government could not concede extensive powers.

Holland. Local retail trade was effectively in the hands of the Chinese. For these reasons he was not disinclined to hope that, after independence, the State could be the agent whose power could protect him, which could break the power of foreign monopoly, and which could foster a truly "Indonesianized economy." This phenomenon of a business class supporting a socialistically inclined nationalist movement was not a purely Indonesian one. Wertheim sees it as part of a more general Asian pattern. Whereas in Europe the rise of a bourgeoisie led to the flourishing of an individualist outlook, and in economic terms, to a competitive laissez-faire capitalism, the Asian bourgeoisie "arrived on the scene too late to realize to the full its tendencies in the direction of individualism." [24] Where monopoly rather than the competition between private businessmen was the rule, a different kind of challenge was required, and the collectivist element in nationalist thought was therefore not repugnant.

This was, of course, very much a matter of degree. There were individualist elements in nationalism as well as socialist elements, and there was a clear difference of emphasis between the social philosophy, in particular, of the merchant whose Islamic faith had been influenced by modernist teaching and that of the Western-educated civil servant, usually Javanese, whose principal frustration was that he could not secure an administrative position commensurate with his talents. This contrast between differing types within the broad stream of the nationalist movement is close to that of Feith's broad opposition between the Islamic-entrepreneurial political culture and the Javanese-aristocratic political culture. A representative of the former was aware of the realities of economic activity in a way that a representative of the latter was not. He might not have possessed the initiative, even after independence had been achieved, to break through the limits of small-scale rural trade and to pioneer an economic revolution. He was on the other hand likely to display a more pragmatic and more individualist outlook than would be shown by a member of the Indonesian white collar middle class. The interests of the latter were theoretical and political. He looked to political independence as offering the way to power and was ready to assume that problems of economic development could be handled by an independent state without great difficulty. Such an emphasis was in part, perhaps, the result of education and of occupa-

---

[24] Wertheim, *Indonesian Society in Transition*, p. 47.

tion. But it sprang in part also from a deeper cultural source—from a traditional Javanese concern with forms rather than with content, with institutions rather than with the policies to be implemented through them. The Javanese leaders of the nationalist movement might have been "new men"—self-consciously so indeed—but they had not entirely severed their ties with a Javanese past.

For the time being these were differences merely in emphasis. While independence was still a distant goal the ideological differences within the nationalist movement were muted. The major divisions that separated the Communist Party from the rest, and which, from the late 1920s were apparent between Moslems and secular nationalists, were important divisions. But apart from these, the very general character of the movement's political and social aspirations enabled a broadly similar outlook to establish itself.

Division and Rivalry

A broad similarity of outlook did not mean a united movement. The history of organized nationalism in Indonesia is a history of a multiplicity of societies able to enter loose alliances from time to time, but more frequently drawing apart from each other, splitting and regrouping. Some of these divisive tendencies, as already remarked, followed genuine lines of cleavage within nationalist thought and outlook, and were therefore entirely to be expected. Sarekat Islam, for example, was prepared for a start to accept within its ranks the Social Democratic Association, but the alliance was a marriage of temporary convenience only. The Communists under the leadership of Semaun[25] and Tan Malaka[26] remained a party within a party and their attempt to seize control of Sarekat Islam, and from there to take over the radical leadership of the nationalist movement as a whole, made a split inevitable. The conflict came to a head in 1921 at the Sixth National Congress of Sarekat Islam, when Communist power within the organization was broken, and the PKI withdrew. Similarly the subsequent estrangement between Moslem societies and others reflected a deepening gulf between clearly opposing points of view. These were in a sense natural divisions. They had their origins in differences of organization and outlook.

[25] See above, Note 20.

[26] Tan Malaka, a Minangkabau school teacher who had been educated in Europe, became a leading figure in the Communist movement soon after its foundation. He was later to oppose the PKI plans for revolt in 1926 and to break with the official party and form his own movement.

Again the formation in 1913 of the separate Eurasian party, Insulinde, had some point in that it represented a distinct ethnic interest. But there were other divisions that did not appear to be based on interest or ideology—divisions among those who could be regarded as representative of the broad stream of secular nationalism—and these were harder to explain.

Organized nationalism may be regarded as beginning in 1908 with the society Boedi Oetomo, but this organization was concerned with cultural rather than with political goals and its appeal was to the educated rather than to the mass of society. Sarekat Islam was formed four years later and was quite a different affair almost from the beginning. Though it arose originally out of an association of Javanese traders concerned to resist Chinese penetration into the batik industry,[27] it was quickly transformed under the chairmanship of Umar Sayed Tjokroaminoto[28] into a mass political party with a strong agitational character. Until its split with the Communist Party in the early 1920s, Sarekat Islam constituted the vanguard of the nationalist movement and up to this time a reasonable degree of unity had been maintained. After the split, however, and after the defeat of the subsequent abortive Communist revolts of 1926 and 1927, the fissiparous tendencies of the nationalist movement began to assert themselves, and a variety of new organizations appeared on the scene. One of these, the Nationalist party (PNI) formed in 1927, did show signs of providing a new and dynamic leadership.[29] Under the guidance of its chairman, Sukarno, it grew rapidly in size and took the initiative in attempting to draw other nationalist societies into one organization. A loose federation of parties (PPPKI) was in fact formed, but it lacked real coherence and, though it survived the banning of the PNI and the arrest of Sukarno in 1929, it lost its momentum thereby. PNI's members, after the outlawing of their party, were absorbed by the Indonesian People's Party (PRI) and the Indonesian Party (Partindo). Among this cluster of organizations

[27] Batik is a patterned cloth produced by dyeing material onto which the patterns have been waxed. The designs are usually based on traditional motifs and the industry was regarded as a peculiarly Javanese preserve.

[28] Tjokroaminoto was of aristocratic origins and had been trained for governmental service. He was thus representative of many Indonesian intellectuals who preferred a career of political activism.

[29] This party was not the same as the Nationalist Party (PNI) of the Independent Republic. The latter was founded in 1946. Though it assumed the old name, and in fact contained many of those who had founded the original party, it was nonetheless a new organization.

there were differences of view as to the best means of pursuing the common goal. PNI had adopted a radical line of opposition to the government and Partindo followed broadly in its footsteps. Similar attitudes were reflected in the Freedom Group (later called the Indonesian National Education Club) but this organization was more elitist in character and devoted itself, under the inspiration of Sjahrir and Hatta, to the task of training a leadership for nationalist activity. PRI, by contrast, was more moderate and aimed at achieving independence through cooperation with the Dutch. So did the Greater Indonesia Party (Parindra), formed in 1935, which was willing to work within the framework of the Volksraad. A more radical party—the Indonesian People's Movement (Gerindo)—was formed in 1937. A new attempt was made to unify the nationalist movement as a whole in 1939. In that year a new Federation of Indonesian Political Parties (Gapi) was formed, but the outbreak of World War II, and the German invasion of the Netherlands in the following year, prevented any test of its effectiveness, and it began to fall apart shortly before the Japanese invasion of Java.[30]

Division and rivalry thus seem to have been characteristic of Indonesian nationalism. It is significant that even under the Japanese occupation, and subsequently during the revolution itself, the movement was still not able to attain organizational unity. Why should this have been so? Why was even secular nationalism in Indonesia never able to mobilize its struggle for independence within the framework of a single organization similar, for example, to the Indian Congress Party? The question is not easy to answer. The reason may lie in part in the character of Dutch rule and in the nature of the Netherlands' attitude to the nationalist movement itself.

The Indies Government was uncertain in its handling of nationalism, alternating between tolerance and repression. Awakening political consciousness, it could be argued, was a proper consequence of the educational policies of the Ethical System, and in this frame of mind the government was able to view the formation of Boedi Oetomo without too much concern. Sarekat Islam, with its more radical outlook, was another matter. After this organization had demonstrated, in remarkable fashion, its ability to attract mass support, the Government reacted by recognizing its branches but

---

[30] The best short treatment of the course of the nationalist movement in the 1920s and 1930s may be found in Kahin, op. cit., Chapter III.

refusing to recognize its central headquarters. Whether this was designed to immobilize the organization or, as Van Niel argues,[31] was intended as a benevolent move to protect it from the possibility of prosecution, may be a matter of debate, but there were certainly differences of opinion within the Indies administration as to the dangers of the organization. With the formation of the Volksraad, the Government hoped that nationalist feeling would be diverted into legitimate channels and that a great deal of its sting would be removed in consequence. In fact, the Volksraad provided a forum for extremely vigorous criticism, which caught the Government off balance and which led to the promise of further, though still limited, political reforms. After that, official policy tended rather more in the direction of repression than of tolerance. The Communist revolts of 1926-27 seemed to justify firmness. Their suppression was accompanied by large scale arrests and by the exile of a considerable number of political prisoners to Boven Digul in New Guinea.[32] Thereafter the arrest from time to time of such leaders as Sukarno, Hatta, and Sjahrir reflected a determination to check all radical criticism.[33] But even then the Government did not mobilize sufficient force to crush the nationalist movement thoroughly. Had it tried to do so, this might have created a sufficient sense of urgency to close nationalist ranks. An outlawed nationalism forced to work underground might well have developed a tightly organized political machine able to impose a firm discipline on its members. Conversely the indecisiveness and inconsistency of government action permitted, and possibly even encouraged, a variety of organizations to compete with one another.

The elitist character of the nationalist leadership and the gap between leaders and their mass following may have contributed to the situation. It was perhaps natural that a small intellectual and administrative leadership should tend to be schismatic. Though its members shared a broadly similar outlook, and represented much the same kind of interest, their road to influence and power depended upon their ability to mobilize mass support, and in the process minor differences of emphasis were likely to be magnified into major differences

---

[31] Van Niel, *op. cit.*, p. 96.

[32] 1300 were arrested and 823 sent to New Guinea (Feith, *op. cit.*, p. 4).

[33] Sukarno was arrested in 1929, released in 1931, and arrested again and exiled in 1933.

of principle. Cliques and factions were thus an obstacle to the formation of even a loosely organized unity.

Fruits of the Japanese Occupation

The increasing firmness displayed by the Dutch during the 1930s was quite sufficient to keep nationalism under control for the time being. The colonial regime was still able to mobilize more than enough force to preserve with ease its own authority, and presumably it could have continued to do so indefinitely if it had not been for the cataclysm of the Japanese invasion. The defeat of the Dutch represented not merely the destruction of a system of power. Psychologically its importance lay in the blow to Dutch prestige. Dutch authority had depended, not just on the crude application of physical force, but upon the cooperation of important traditional elements within the Indonesian community. The ability thus to command the loyalty of some Indonesians was shattered forever by the sudden collapse of the colonial regime under the Japanese advance.

The Japanese occupation was not a simple substitution of one colonial regime for another. It provided a totally new environment within which the forces of Indonesian resistance could grow more rapidly to maturity. Having destroyed the apparatus of Dutch power, the Japanese were confronted with the immediate task of keeping the wheels of routine administration turning and, in the long run, with the need to find some sort of basis in consent for their own regime. Their solutions to the two problems were to have important consequences for the future. For the first task, the obvious expedient was to use Indonesian civil servants, though these were kept firmly under Japanese control. For the second, the Japanese in due course recognized the necessity of coming to terms with nationalist leaders in the hope of mobilizing their support for the occupation.

Certainly though the Japanese were compelled in this way to do business with the leaders of the nationalist movement, they wished to do so very much on their own terms. Nationalism was, for the time being, to be the servant of occupation policy; not until the tide of the Pacific war had turned decisively against them did the Japanese take practical steps to prepare for the establishment of an independent Indonesia, and then, of course, only in order to embarrass the returning Allies. But even in the earlier stages they were unable to control the forces that they set in motion. The use for propaganda purposes of prominent figures, including Sukarno himself, was intended to reduce opposition to Japanese authority. In fact it gave such leaders a vantage point from which radical nationalist consciousness could be developed among the masses of the population.[34] In other respects, too, Japanese policy consolidated nationalist feeling. The creation of an all-embracing Moslem organization comprising Muhammadiyah, Nahdatul Ulama and other groups, was intended to make for more effective control of Moslem feeling. In practical terms it laid a foundation for united Moslem political activity, which was to carry over into the early years of independence.

While closing some fissures, Japanese policy at the same time opened new ones within the nationalist movement. Divisions between Moslem organizations and the secular nationalist leaders were widened. Divisions established themselves also between those who collaborated and those, such as Sjahrir, whose wartime role was to lay the framework of an underground movement.[35]

As the war proceeded, the increasing harshness and arrogance of Japanese rule gave Indonesians a glimpse of a more thoroughgoing imperialism than that of the Dutch. Under pressure of coming defeat, the Japanese set up a Preparatory Committee to prepare a draft constitution for independence. But with the Japanese surrender to the Allies in August 1945, the nationalist leaders, under pressure from elements anxious to avoid acquiring independence as a gift from the Japanese, themselves declared Indonesia to be an independent republic.[36] A government was set up under Sukarno's presidency, and when British troops, forming the spearhead of the Allied advance, landed in Java, they found a functioning administration in existence. Shortly afterward, Dutch troops began to arrive to reclaim, as they thought, their country's rightful possession, and the stage was set for the revo-

[34] The Dutch were later to level a collaborationist charge against Sukarno. Notice Kahin's argument (op. cit., pp. 104ff.) that in fact he used his opportunities during the occupation to preach a nationalism that was anti-Western, certainly, but also, by clear implication, anti-Japanese. But note also Benda's criticism of this interpretation (op. cit., pp. 174-75 and 277).

[35] Feith, op. cit., p. 22.

[36] There have been differences of opinion as to the exact details of the circumstances leading to the proclamation of independence. For an analysis of the two crucial days before August 17, 1945, see Benedict R. O'G. Anderson, Some Aspects of Indonesian Politics under the Japanese Occupation: 1944-1945 (Cornell Modern Indonesia Project, Interior Report Series, Ithaca, 1961), Chapter VI. See also S. Nishijima and K. Kishi, Japanese Military Administration in Indonesia (translation prepared by U.S. Dept. of Commerce, Joint Publications Research Service, 1963), Chapter VII.

lutionary struggle that fluctuated between negotiation and open conflict for the next four years.

Nationalism Since 1945

The details of the final struggle for independence—of the negotiations leading to the ambiguous Linggadjati Agreement, of the first
police action, of the United Nations intervention, the Renville Truce,
and the second police action—need not concern us here. The story
has been brilliantly told elsewhere,[37] and it is sufficient to notice several general points.

The Indonesian victory was not won by the Republic's own unaided
efforts. Political help from outside, expressed in the United Nations
intervention and in the ultimate American decision to bring pressure
to bear on the Dutch, was of vital importance. So also was the general
climate of international opinion. The British concession of independence to India and the growing pressure of nationalist feeling in African colonies were indications that a new world was coming into
existence. But still, the determined efforts of the Indonesian forces,
even if they were not sufficient in themselves to bring victory, were
sufficient to prevent the Dutch from reimposing their own rule. As
General Nasution was later to say:

> The reason that the Dutch were finally willing to withdraw their
> forces from Indonesia was not because they were defeated by our army,
> but because they were weakened and stymied by us so that there was no
> longer any hope for them to destroy the Republic. When their efforts
> to do this were frustrated, international pressure hastened the transfer
> of sovereignty.[38]

In conducting this struggle the nationalist movement did not remain completely united. As we have already indicated, the schismatic
character of prewar nationalism was still to be observed, even while
the energies of the self-proclaimed Republic were devoted to a struggle for mere survival. In part, the internal rifts that revealed themselves between 1945 and 1949 were the product of Communist initiative, culminating in the Madiun affair in 1948. Ostensibly the issue
at stake on this occasion was how much should be conceded by the
government of the Republic in its negotiations with the Dutch. But
underlying the overt issue was a bid for power on the part of the Com-

---

[37] Kahin, *op. cit.*
[38] A. H. Nasution, *Fundamentals of Guerilla Warfare* (Djakarta, 1953), p. 15.

munist Party occurring within the context of the sharpening of international Communist doctrine. Popular fronts were now out of favor
and, in the view of Communist theory, the world was divided into
only two camps. Increasing intransigence on the part of the Communist parties of Indonesia, China, Malaya, and the Philippines was
a uniform consequence of the two-camps doctrine. In addition to the
deep gulf between Communists and others, there remained, in non-
Communist ranks, a multiplicity of parties and organizations which
maneuvered for position even during the struggle with the Dutch.
Even before independence, therefore, Indonesia had acquired the
essentials of a multi-party system with all the elements of weakness
which that entailed.

In spite of the existence of a wide variety of organizations and
groups, it did not prove possible for the Dutch, in their efforts to
reimpose their authority, to split the nationalist movement. An attempt was made to do just this. The natural lines of division in Dutch
eyes appeared to coincide with lines of geographical and ethnic difference. In particular, the Dutch advocacy of a federal constitution
for an independent Indonesia seemed likely to capitalize on the widespread suspicion of Javanese dominance that was to be found in the
outer islands. The persistence of traditional aristocracies in the indirectly ruled areas outside the island of Java also offered the possibility
of playing upon fears of extreme republicanism that might follow a
Java-led bid for independence. The Dutch attempt to balance the
more numerous Javanese by insisting on a federal Indonesia as a basis
for negotiation was thus likely to strike a sympathetic chord in
Celebes, the Lesser Sundas, and Sumatra. If this was an early possibility, it was to be destroyed by the Netherlands' own actions. The
states established by the Dutch as suitable constituent members of a
federation were given no real responsibilities of government and
proved to be little more than puppets,[39] and ultimately the second
Dutch police action had the effect of closing nationalist ranks and
bringing the outer islands solidly behind the Republic.

The fact that Indonesian freedom could be obtained only by open
conflict thus contributed to a new sense of national solidarity extending well beyond the bounds of prewar nationalism, but its consequences did not stop there. The revolution was also an emotional
experience of great importance for the future. Freedom through revo-

[39] Kahin, op. cit., Chapter XII, gives a careful study of the degree of genuine
autonomy enjoyed by the governments of these states.

lution was to be seen by Indonesians in the future as a far more precious freedom than that which some other dependencies obtained more easily through the peaceful withdrawal of their colonial overlords; and the concept of revolution itself was to be made a crucial motif in the Indonesian political outlook. It is not easy to pinpoint the exact meaning of the term. The mere attainment of independence from foreign rule is not in itself a revolution as the word is normally used nowadays, and it is interesting to notice that nationalist thought in the 1920s and 1930s did not make a great deal of play with the revolutionary idea. It was only during the actual struggle that there was a self-conscious insistence upon the concept, with its implication of a change in the structure of society accompanying the change in regime, and with its sense of dedication to the active building of a new order.

In terms of social change and of a genuine transfer of power, there was indeed a revolution during these years. Whereas the Dutch had exerted their power to a considerable extent through traditional channels of authority—through the *priyayi* in Java and through small rulers of varying degrees of importance outside Java—the revolution was to open the way for new men—the products of the Netherlands' own educational policies—and for the activity of new organizations. There were tremendous opportunities, and a vigorous competition for power and prestige, in the vacuum created by the Japanese withdrawal, and the consequent changes in the structure of society and in the patterns of authority might well be termed revolutionary. But the symbolic importance of the revolution was important for its own sake, and in independent Indonesia the consciousness of revolutionary origins was to remain as a matter of national pride. Much of this feeling was artificially maintained. During the late 1950s and early 1960s, the concept of revolution was used very much as a propaganda device through which appeals could be made for the preservation of national unity against the dangers of internal dissension. But beneath the political manipulation there existed a genuine pride in achievement and a genuine sense of a continuing struggle to be conducted with the same unity of purpose as was the struggle against the Dutch.

Yet, while the idea of revolution continued to be an evocative symbol, there were to be important shifts of emphasis within it. During the period of actual conflict, and in the following few years, revolution meant innovation and implied a rejection of, or at least a lack of interest in, the remoter sources of Indonesian culture. "Westernization" rather than simply "modernization" was the goal. As we have seen, this was in line with the largely Western outlook of the nationalist movement from its early years. At least the emphasis was placed on political democracy and the creation (by means not clearly specified) of a just and prosperous society forming part of a world-wide industrial civilization rather than upon the continuity of Indonesian civilization. But as the 1950s proceeded, a growing emphasis was to be placed on the need for a specifically Indonesian identity, and it was the turn of Western values to suffer rejection. Liberal democracy was now held to be alien to the Indonesian spirit, and an important element in Sukarno's campaign for Guided Democracy was his claim that it embodied the cohesion and the sense of common concern to be found within the Indonesian village. In economic terms the nationalist demand for the "Indonesianization" of the economy found practical expression in the expulsion of the Dutch in 1957 and the addition of the idea of "Indonesian socialism" to the ideas of Guided Democracy and Indonesian identity. To some extent this desire for "a personality" and the accompanying emphasis on the importance of an indigenous cultural tradition was a self-conscious nativism, deliberately fostered, but to some extent it reflected the fact that social changes over half a century, accelerated as they had been under the influence of European industrial society, had still disturbed only in part the complex mixture of tradition already existing. Indonesian nationalism, in attempting to build a new society, had to come to terms in some degree with the inertia of indigenous patterns.

SEVEN

INDONESIA SINCE INDEPENDENCE

1949-1964

The second Dutch police action, launched in December 1948, was intended to crush Indonesian resistance once and for all. Its effect, instead, was to rally world opinion to the support of the Republic, to provoke a more determined United Nations intervention than had been possible before, and to lead to a crystallization of the American attitude in Indonesia's favor. Under these various pressures the Netherlands finally found it necessary to give way. Between August and November 1949 a round table conference between the Netherlands, the Republic, and representatives of the various states that had been set up as part of the Dutch plans for a federal Indonesia was held at The Hague to prepare the way to independence. The round table agreements contained certain compromises. The question of West New Guinea was reserved for later negotiation, and remained to plague Dutch–Indonesian relations for thirteen years. Indonesia agreed to take over the debts of the former colony, and she gave certain guarantees to Dutch investments in her territory. A federal constitution for a United States of Indonesia was agreed to. The agreements also looked forward to continuing cooperation between the Netherlands and the Republic within the framework of a Netherlands–Indonesian Union. The crucial clauses, however, provided for the establishment of a sovereign independent state, able to make its own decisions on the nature of its future cooperation with the Netherlands as on all other aspects of national policy.

After the formal transfer of sovereignty, Indonesia faced the future with the momentum of her revolution to carry her forward but with latent problems of national cohesion still to be solved. Some of these were the products of the recent experience of colonial rule and some had their origins much further back in her past. The government of the infant republic had to conciliate its subjects in a way that the Dutch had not. It had to establish its authority upon the real bases of power in the community, and only experience could show where these lay. The early years were therefore inevitably years of experiment in which the parliamentary institutions with which the Republic began its existence were tried in practice, modified, and eventually discarded when they failed to correspond with the emerging realities of the political situation.

Failures of Liberal Democracy

To understand these developments it is necessary to observe briefly the character of political life as it existed during these early years of independence. The outward forms were to change dramatically after 1955, but the seeds of later development were visible before then.

Constitutional forms in any situation at best bear only a rough correspondence to political realities—to the way in which the major forces operate and to the procedures by which the major decisions are in fact made. But during the first six years of independence it may be said that the correspondence between forms and reality was much closer than it was later to become. The constitution provided for parliamentary government, with a system of cabinet responsibility, and, in consequence, for a comparatively weak presidency, and political power was articulated principally through political parties. These were not the only political forces in the country. If a crude classification may be permitted at this point, several other forces must be recognized in addition to the specifically "political" organizations. The Army obviously possessed the power to play an independent role if it so desired and could agree on a particular course, and no government could survive in the face of active opposition from a united Army leadership. The president himself, in spite of the constitutional limits of his power, enjoyed a prestige that would have supported a strong and independent role had he chosen to play it. Some of the regions outside Java had watched with some suspicion the dismantling of the federal constitution and could bring a direct pressure to bear on the central government. But in fact, during the early years, these extraconstitutional elements pressed their demands through parties and the civil service, and allowed the formal operation of parliamentary democracy. The Army chose to regard itself with great propriety as the professional arm of a civil government, except where it felt that professional issues were at stake. The president, in spite of his considerable finesse as a politician (or perhaps because of it), accepted his constitutional role of national figurehead with only minor exceptions. Though his personal prestige enabled him to wield a greater influence than was proper for a president in a parliamentary democracy, his intervention for the most part was not yet an overt intervention.[1] And for the time being the regions accepted their position within the unitary state and looked forward to the concession of a degree of autonomy within that framework as meeting their major demands. In these circumstances the road to power appeared to lie through party activity, and the parties were to a marked extent under the control of a narrow leadership representing Indonesia's Western-educated elite.

From the outset Indonesia possessed a wide range of parties, a fact that made it a foregone conclusion that proportional representation would be adopted as the basis of the country's electoral system, thus in turn ensuring the continuance of a multi-party system. Approximately thirty parties in fact contested the election of 1955. However this array of groups was dominated by four major parties whose leadership was clearly confirmed by the elections. The position of Islam as the overwhelmingly predominant religion in the country was reflected in the fact that two of the big four were Moslem parties—Masjumi and Nahdatul Ulama (NU). The remaining two were the Nationalist Party (Partai Nasional Indonesia—PNI) and the Communist Party (Partai Kommunis Indonesia—PKI). Of the lesser parties the most important by far was the Socialist Party (Partai Sosialis Indonesia—PSI), a party with very strong intellectual support and commanding the loyalty of many of the country's senior public servants, but with no great popular support. The PSI was virtually eliminated in the elections—a fact that was symptomatic of impending changes in Indonesia's total political life. The two Christian parties—Protestant (Parkindo) and Catholic, and two smaller Islamic parties—PSII and Perti, were not unimportant and a variety of other groups vaguely "nationalist" in character brought up the rear.

[1] For a discussion of the position of the president under the 1950 Constitution, see George McT. Kahin, ed., *Major Governments of Asia* (New York, 1958), pp. 542-45. See also A. K. Pringgodigdo, *The Office of President in Indonesia as Defined in the Three Constitutions in Theory and Practice* (Cornell Modern Indonesia Project, Translation Series, Ithaca, 1957).

The nature of the interests represented by the major parties and the character of the competition between them were not very clearly defined. Party rivalry was obviously not, in the Indonesian setting, a class rivalry, though some elements of class difference may be distinguished in respective party followings. Masjumi tended to find its support in small market towns rather than the countryside, and in regions outside Java where a greater degree of indigenous Indonesian commercial activity was to be found—in western Sumatra and southern Sulawesi for example. While it would be wrong to regard it as representing commercial interests, it did have this element present in contrast to Nahdatul Ulama (NU), whose strength was to be found in the countryside. Masjumi, it should be added, represented a more modernist version of Islam—an Islam that had tried to come to terms with Western thinking—while NU remained more traditional and conservative. The Nationalist Party (PNI), while seeking support from all elements, had a strong hold in some parts of the civil service. The Ministry of Information for a time was almost a PNI preserve, and the party also had influential supporters in the ranks of the territorial administrative service. Finally the Communist Party (PKI), though it did have its obvious field of operations in labor unions and controlled the largest of the labor federations, the All-Indonesia Central Labor Organization (Sentral Organisasi Buruh Seluruh Indonesia—SOBSI), did not neglect its opportunities among the rural population. Through its Peasant Front (Barisan Tani Indonesia—BTI) its grass roots organization proved remarkably effective.

If the first three of these parties did not represent clearly distinct interest groups, neither was there any sharp difference in program among them, and they managed to forge a rough basis of cooperation in the pre-election years. All cabinets at this stage were based on some combination of these three with lesser parties also sharing in the spoils, though there were elements of a broad opposition between Masjumi and its supporters on the one hand and PNI and its supporters on the other. Masjumi, perhaps more in touch with economic realities and more willing to accept the principle of foreign investment, represented more moderate domestic policies and was suspicious of Sukarno's later willingness to cooperate with the Communist Party. Like the Socialist Party it was more attached to liberal democratic institutions, more sensitive to the dangers of Javanese political dominance—and also, like the Socialist Party, was eventually to find itself in opposition to the president and his supporters. The Nationalist Party regarded itself as the custodian of nationalist feeling, but the successful outcome of the revolutionary struggle left it without a clear cause to fight for. Nationalism in the post-revolutionary era was confined pretty much to a program of "Indonesianization" of the economy at the expense of Chinese and remaining Dutch interests, and to the advocacy of a neutralist foreign policy.

These policy differences, however, were not really sharp enough to suggest an analysis of political life in terms of party rivalry based on differences of program and interest. In a sense it might be said that Masumi and NU were rivals in that they competed for the support of the same group—the devout Moslem population. In the same way PNI and PKI appealed to the non-Moslem or nominally Moslem *abangan* element in Java. (The PKI success in the 1955 elections when they increased their representation from 17 to 39 seats, and their further advance in the regional elections of 1957, appeared to have been achieved at the expense of PNI.) But these did not represent, in any ordinary sense, interest groups, and party attempts to capture support in particular areas centered on their efforts to win the support of influential individuals rather than in attempting systematically to represent interests.[2] It should be noted also that the major parties were unevenly distributed throughout the archipelago. All found significant electoral support in Java, but NU, PNI, and PKI were primarily Java-based parties while Masjumi's main centers of strength were outside Java, particularly in western Sumatra and southern Sulawesi. For this reason party conflicts tended to take on a regional—and indeed an ethnic—flavor. Masjumi in particular tended to become identified with an anti-Javanese outlook. (It should be noted that in Java Masjumi's strength lay chiefly in West Java—*i.e.*, the area of Sudanese, not the Javanese ethnic group.)

Through the agency of parties of this general character parliamentary democracy in Indonesia developed its own distinctive modes of operation and displayed, also, its own distinctive weaknesses. A multi-party system in any case militated against strong and stable government, and Indonesia's series of coalitions could operate only on the basis of their lowest common denominators. This was accentuated by the absence of sharply defined differences between parties,

[2] See Soedjatmoko, "The Role of Political Parties in Indonesia," in Philip W. Thayer, ed., *Nationalism and Progress in Free Asia* (Baltimore, 1956).

by the existence of distinct factions within parties and by the absence of party discipline, which together made the loyalty of individuals a doubtful quantity. As a symptom of the lack of discipline, the possibility of differences developing between parliamentary leadership and the parties' extraparliamentary executives also stood in the way of the development of firm party policies. (That the PKI was a notable exception in all these respects goes without saying.) The weakness of political leadership was accentuated also by the characteristically Indonesian desire to negotiate the widest possible area of agreement among diverse groups for the making of important decisions. Controversial issues tended to be withdrawn from the floor of the House until party managers could iron out major differences and secure by discussion a measure of agreement.

More serious perhaps than all these flaws was the inevitable inability of any post-revolutionary government to satisfy the popular expectations following nationalist victory. The Dutch domination was blamed for all the evils of the colonial era: its removal was expected to usher in a golden age. But in fact Indonesia's general economic situation, her dependence on foreign markets for a handful of staple exports, her need for foreign capital, remained substantially unchanged, and indeed shortage of technical and administrative skills affected her ability even to retain prewar levels of prosperity. These were fundamental facts. Reference is often made by observers to Indonesia's great potential wealth, but when her enormous pressure of numbers is set against her resources, the picture of a wealthy country tends to evaporate. Of great importance too was the existence of regional suspicion of any central government, a fact that made the normal operation of a party system within the framework of parliamentary institutions a hazardous matter at best.

Against the background of these general considerations there occurred shifts in the balance of Indonesia's political forces. Within the party system itself the approach of the first national elections had important consequences for the nature of party activity and organization. The need to bid for electoral support forced at least a temporary concentration on organizational matters, increased the importance of the lower echelons of the parties, and gave scope for the talent of a different type of leadership. Electoral needs, in effect, helped to undermine the existing intellectual leadership and affected the general consensus between leaders of all parties on which political activity had hitherto been based. The elections themselves,

though an outstanding success in certain respects, were followed
within a year by signs of the growing importance of extraparliamentary forces. From his vantage point as president, and on the basis
of his prestige as a revolutionary nationalist leader, Sukarno began
to allow a freer rein to his undoubted talents for political maneuver.
At the same time the Army, in the persons first of all of individual
commanders, began to intervene directly in the political arena.
These developments foreshadowed the gradual emergence of a new
alignment of forces in Indonesia, in which the President and a
united Army would form the poles of the country's principal political axis.

The Army in 1956 was not united. Indonesia was divided into
seven military regions, two in Sumatra, three in Java, one in Borneo,
and one covering the eastern islands of the archipelago. Troops
tended to have a strong identification with the area to which they
belonged, and their loyalty was, in the first instance, to their
individual commander rather than to the more remote higher command in Djakarta or to the nation as a whole. Thus military commanders had a considerable measure of independence in military
matters, and they also possessed the power to influence the civil
government of their regions. In some areas the writ of the central
government ran, if it ran at all, by the sufferance of the local commander, and the growth of barter trade between Sumatra or Sulawesi
and Singapore or Manila was carried on with the knowledge and, in
some cases, under the direct supervision, of the Army. Indonesian
unity in the mid-1950s was based on an acceptance of these plain
facts and was purchased at the price of official or semi-official
recognition of some local military independence. The government,
and its chief of staff, approved what they could not prevent. The
task of the latter, indeed, was largely a diplomatic one—to seek
through delicate consultations some agreement about regional military cooperation with the center.

In 1956 there were signs that the political influence of the Army
in the regions was to flow over into the sphere of central politics.
In August the Commander of the West Java military region ordered
the arrest of Roeslan Abdulgani, foreign minister, on a charge of
corruption. The minister was released on the intervention of the
prime minister, Ali Sastroamidjojo, and later submitted to an investigation of the charge by a cabinet commission. In November of the
same year Colonel Zulkifli Lubis, Deputy Chief of Staff, attempted

to bring about a coup d'état in Djakarta by seizing control of the city and overthrowing the PNI-dominated government. The plot was discovered in advance and frustrated, but it was significant of a new trend. In December Lt. Col. Husein, regimental commander of Padang, overturned the existing civil administration of the province of Central Sumatra and transferred power to a council representing military and veteran elements. A similar coup in North Sumatra had only a very short lived success.

These signs of military dissatisfaction with the course of parliamentary government provided the environment within which Sukarno was able to play a new personal role. In 1957 he stepped more openly than before into the political arena and introduced an early version of his plan for guided democracy. He handled with great skill the immediate opposition which resulted, and he thereafter maintained a continuing initiative, in spite of the open revolt in 1958 of west Sumatra and north Sulawesi. The revolt in effect at once revealed the failure of parliamentary democracy and confirmed the emergence of a new balance of power. It constituted a crisis in which Sukarno enjoyed unusual freedom for maneuver. At the same time it created a rival with whom his power was of necessity to be shared. The Army in suppressing the rebellion gained a new unity and a new prestige which, at the very least, made it an arbiter of domestic politics. And political party prestige declined in equal measure.

The character of this development must now be examined more closely, but it may be said, at this point, that the failure of the experiment in liberal democracy was not accidental. Even in the first years of independence, while political parties served as the main agents of political activity, they held this position as much by the grace of other forces as by their own genuine strength. The latter was as yet untested, but even so, with the advantage of hindsight, it is clear that party strengths and party rivalries did not reflect accurately the real distribution of power in the country. This was made plain in the crisis of 1956-59, and the crisis further accentuated the gap between constitutional forms and political realities.

Transition to Guided Democracy

Sukarno had already indicated his dissatisfaction with liberal political theory in a speech of October 28, 1956, in which he had condemned the selfishness of political parties that were inclined to put their own interests before those of the country, and he had called upon the parties to "bury themselves"—an invitation which, for the time being, they declined to accept. In 1957, against the background of incipient regional revolts, in particular the establishment of a separatist provincial government in west Sumatra, Sukarno advanced for the first time his own solution, which he was to continue to advocate with skill and persistence until he was in a position, two years later, to secure its adoption. Sukarno's plan, or "conception" as he called it, was certainly not a blue print for action. He was probably never at any stage entirely clear about what it was that he wanted, and his plans reflected a mood as much as a program. Very briefly his proposals in their original form, as we have already noticed in Chapter I, were concerned with the creation of political machinery that would express what he considered to be the basic principles of Indonesia's way of life—the principles of deliberation and consensus *musjawarah* and *mufakat*. These principles were held to represent the sort of procedures that existed in their ideal form at the village level. Decisions in the village, he argued, were not reached by debate and majority vote. Rather they resulted from prolonged discussion and the gradual emergence of something approaching a sense of the meeting. If no such consensus emerged no decision would be made. According to Sukarno these basic principles should serve as the model for national politics as well as for village affairs.

One may wonder whether the idea of consensus was really a distinctive Indonesian principle, and whether it did represent the nature of decision-making at the village level. Other societies, too, have their informal methods of securing the widest measure of agreement before engaging in the formal discussion of a proposal in councils or parliaments. But it is true in Indonesia that exceptional efforts are made to avoid a formal vote which crystallizes differences, brings conflict into the open, and makes withdrawal difficult to obtain. Indonesia's council and parliamentary procedures do show a desire to prolong discussion, a determination to preserve flexibility as long as possible, a great emphasis on harmony rather than conflict. In any case, translated into practical terms, these principles involved, in 1957, two main proposals. The President desired first of all a cabinet based on the participation of all major political groups including the Communist Party, which had hitherto been excluded from all post-independence cabinets but was now, he argued, too important a force to be ignored. Secondly he urged the formation of a National Council under his own chairmanship and representing all major interests within the community—workers, peasants, religious groups, women, youth, citizens of foreign descent, the various regions of the country. Such a council he considered should enable all significant opinions to be represented; and a consensus achieved through deliberation in such an assembly, should, he felt, express a common national will and command as a result an unchallenged authority. The council was to represent the community as a whole, just as a cabinet would represent and reflect the whole composition of parliament.

Sukarno's proposals evoked hostility from many quarters. The Moslem parties objected to cooperation with the PKI. Military commanders in East Indonesia, Kalimantan, Atjeh, and South Sumatra assumed control of the administration in their respective provinces and awaited the further turn of events. The cabinet resigned and a state of emergency was declared. The final outcome fell short of the President's plan. Though a new cabinet was formed under the former Minister of Planning, Dr. Djuanda, it was not the "four-legged" cabinet (PNI–Masjumi–NU–PKI) desired by Sukarno. It was theoretically nonparty, though it did in fact have representatives of parties and included two Communist sympathizers. A National Council was established representing the various functional groups, but it was constituted as an advisory body only. At the same time, though it was not to be apparent until later, these events did reflect a shift in the country's internal balance of power; the direct intervention of the President in politics, the action of regional commanders, and the hesitancy of political party leadership were all signs of future developments.

It is not necessary to detail the subsequent steps by which these signs were confirmed into a clear trend. Of great importance was the stepping up of the West Irian campaign and, in the course of that campaign, the take-over of Dutch property in Indonesia. The take-overs were initiated by workers, but they were followed within a few days by Army action to take control of these enterprises. The formal establishment in subsequent months of a government-controlled, army-managed estates system was of vital importance for the economic future of the country. Finally on February 15, 1958, Indonesia was faced with a much more open division than ever before in the form of a rebel movement in West Sumatra, which set up "the Revolutionary Government of the Republic of Indonesia" (Pemerintah Revolusioner Republik Indonesia—PRRI), charged

Sukarno with leading the country toward Communism, and appealed to the outside world for recognition as the government of Indonesia. North Sulawesi aligned itself with the rebel government. This open challenge was met successfully by military action during the course of 1958 and early 1959, as a result of which Army prestige and, in particular, the prestige of the Chief of Staff, General Nasution, was greatly enhanced. Early in 1959 President Sukarno returned once again, but this time in more thoroughgoing fashion, to his guided democracy theme. His new approach was embodied, after a great deal of preparatory discussion with political and military leaders, in an appeal for a return to the Constitution of 1945—the constitution which had been adopted by the infant republic after its proclamation of independence. Sukarno's appeal was made, first of all, to the Constituent Assembly which, since its election in 1955, had been engaged in drafting a permanent constitution to replace the 1950 provisional constitution. The Constituent Assembly in due course rejected the appeal and in these circumstances the President dissolved it on July 5, 1959, and introduced the Constitution of 1945 by decree.

The Constitution of 1945 was a much more flexible document than that of 1950. It provided for presidential rather than parliamentary government. During the revolution, as we have seen, it had been operated in a parliamentary manner, but the President's intention, in 1959, was to use it as the basis for a presidential system of government, and its vagueness about details meant that it offered considerable opportunity for an even stronger presidential executive than had, perhaps, been intended by its original drafters. After 1959, within the framework of this constitution, there was erected a complex structure of deliberative machinery that was intended to secure that consensus of opinion on which, in the President's view, policy ought to be based. In the new structure, though a People's Deliberative Assembly (Madjelis Permusjawaratan Rakjat—MPR) was to be the source of sovereignty (it was to be composed of 616 members and was to meet at least every four years to set the main lines of national policy), the important organ for practical purposes was to be the Supreme Advisory Council (Dewan Pertimbangan Agung—DPA). This body, composed of 45 members, thus expressed once again the principle of functional representation through which the important strands of national opinion were to be represented. As a corollary it was clear that parliament (also recast to fit into the new plan) had also suffered a serious loss of prestige. The new appointed chamber (termed a *gotong rojong* or mutual help parliament) was composed of 283 members, of which only 129 were drawn from the parties, the remainder being representatives of functional groups. This was supposed to be a temporary parliament, pending the preparation of a new electoral law under which a new body could be chosen. The preparation of an electoral law proved to be a prolonged process. The changed status of the parties was quickly reflected in an edict designed to "simplify" political parties, reducing their number and subjecting them to a closer executive control. Senior civil servants were required to renounce their party membership and the importance of the parties as a way to power and influence was clearly to be minimal in the future.

The declining importance of the parliament was matched by the declining importance of the cabinet. The construction of a whole series of deliberative bodies, some of them, such as the Supreme Advisory Council and the People's Deliberative Assembly, prescribed by the Constitution of 1945, and others, such as the National Planning Council set up for particular purposes, has diluted the policy-making function of the cabinet. And in 1962 sweeping changes in the character and composition of the cabinet itself also helped to reduce its importance. The number of ministers was increased greatly, and the work of ministries was grouped into eight major fields, each under the supervision of a deputy first minister. This appeared to create a rational hierarchy of ministers with comparatively compact leadership under the control of the president at the apex. In practice the reform meant that many of the junior members became little more than senior administrative officials. And there was not the compensating advantage of a small inner cabinet. Regular cabinet meetings were discontinued and important questions tended to be passed to the President.

A *Personal Dictatorship?*

It is not easy to assess the complicated mechanical arrangements for guided democracy. To many observers these developments have represented a simple trend toward personal dictatorship. Each of the series of steps by which Sukarno, between 1957 and 1960, moved further toward his goal appeared as one more betrayal of liberal principles. Indonesia seemed to fit into precisely the same general pattern as that to be observed in other new republics, where representative institutions had tended to lose their power and where trends toward the formation of a stronger executive could be observed. Sukarno himself appeared to be making a bid for absolute personal power and, in view of his wooing of the extreme left as a means of doing so, to be either an unprincipled opportunist or himself Communist-inspired. Indeed there were some grounds for this view. When Sukarno, in 1956, called on the political parties to bury themselves and attacked the self-seeking of politicians and of political parties in general, he was speaking in an ominously familiar idiom.

Such judgments need to be examined with some care. It is certainly true that the presidential edict by which the Constitution of 1945 was adopted was a measure of dubious constitutional propriety. Leaving that point for the lawyers to debate, it is also the case that the Constitution of 1945 placed no clear limits on his power and opened the way for the arbitrary exercise of presidential authority. There were to be many examples of such arbitrary behavior. The dissolution of an elected parliament and its replacement by an appointed one, the stringent curb placed on party activity and the banning, first of the two major "oppositionist" parties and then of all but ten major parties, the increasing reliance upon legislation by presidential regulation—all reflected the magnitude of the expansion of the president's formal authority and the opportunities now presented for the play of presidential caprice. The vagueness and flexibility of the constitution makes it difficult nowadays to define the limits of constitutional behavior.

In making this point, however, it is important to remember two things, one a matter of theory and the other a matter of hard fact. One should notice Sukarno's own rationale of guided democracy— that it claims to be based on the traditional Indonesian principles of deliberation and consensus and that, in consequence, far from being a dictatorship in disguise it in fact makes the most careful provision for consultation and debate. This rationale must not be brushed aside as a mere talking point. There is no doubt that the President has believed sincerely in the view that government must be based on consensus, and that the desire to secure the fullest consultation has operated even to the point of frustrating decision.

Secondly it must be noticed that, whatever the constitutional niceties of his position, the actual opportunities open for the exercise of the President's personal power have not been unlimited. He has been circumscribed by the political forces surrounding him, if not by the constitution itself, and it may fairly be said that guided democracy in action reflects a precarious balance between authoritarian trends and centrifugal countertendencies. There was, admittedly, some consolidation of political forces as a result of rebellion and civil war. Balancing Sukarno himself there was the new unity and strength of the Army, which still seemed willing to remain as an arbiter of affairs rather than to seek a fuller and more formal responsibility. The banning of Masjumi and the Socialist Party removed the main elements of political opposition, and Army and President in effect formed for a time the poles of the country's principal axis of power. But other forces were not eliminated. The leading political parties have not defended themselves against presidential pressure and it is true that, in consequence, their real power, thus left untested, has obviously diminished. In politics as in athletics lack of exercise makes muscles flabby. The machinery of guided democracy at once reflected and accentuated this erosion of party power. The addition of functional representatives and Army representatives to the membership of the new parliament left the parties simply outnumbered, and in any case parliament's importance in the total scheme of things had declined sharply with the creation of the Supreme Advisory Council and of other deliberative bodies. But for all this, parties still existed and still maintained a foothold in the central organs of government as well as in the regional councils. In particular the PKI, though circumscribed in its activities, still retained its social bases of support and its grass roots organization. And, in spite of the crushing of the 1958 rebellion, regional opinion could not be ignored. Indeed the apparent increase in Javanese predominance which has followed the crushing of revolt may well contain the seeds of future resistance. In the meantime the power of regional military commanders has still permitted them to exercise a limited degree of independence though this was very much less in evidence than formerly. Thus, guided democracy notwithstanding, political power in Indonesia has remained diffused and the exercise of authority has been a matter of the adjustment of forces in actual practice. The Constitution of 1945 has left the rules fairly open for this sort of adjustment. It does not prescribe clearly the procedures of decision making.

In this situation the character of the precarious balance between President and Army was, of course, crucial. The relations between the two were marked by fluctuating tension. The President was unable to ignore the Army's strength and indeed he needed its positive support. The Army, in turn, with its prestige raised by its successful handling of the revolt, exercised wide powers of routine administration under the continuing state of emergency, but it lacked a coherent policy of its own which it would be willing to impose on the country, and it recognized the need to accept the legitimating figure of the President. The two were thus bound in partnership. But it was not always an easy partnership; there were disagreements as well as agreements. Each needed the other but the mutual need was tempered by tension between them. The Army would have liked for example to take firm action to circumscribe the power of the Communists. The President opposed such action, partly because he regarded the PKI as an important constituent of the consensus he was seeking, but partly also because the continued existence of the party gave a fluidity to the whole political situation which added to Sukarno's own freedom of maneuver.

The President–Army axis has not been a fixed and unchanging component of Indonesian politics. By 1963 the Army's lack of positive independent leadership had undermined its own authority, and the ending of the emergency in May 1963 reduced the official military role in day-to-day administration. Of importance too was the fact that the Army did not escape charges of corruption, both in its civil administrative capacity and in the part it had played in the running of government enterprises taken over by the Dutch in 1957, and its prestige as a reforming force declined accordingly. More important was its lack of any clear idea of how to use its power. In these circumstances it was no match for the superior tactical skill of the President, who was able to play upon the existence of factions within the Army, and who was adept in preserving the political initiative in his own hands. By 1963 Sukarno had demonstrated his ability to manipulate the Army as he manipulated other forces. The Army, of course, remained an important power, capable of dramatic intervention in a situation of crisis, but much more of a junior partner than it had been.

In spite of this shift in the balance of domestic politics, the central point of the argument remains—namely that Sukarno, for all his political finesse and for all the formal authority given him under the Constitution, must work within a given situation. His ability to shape it and manipulate it is limited—not by the Constitution certainly, but by other centers of power—and his need to accommodate himself is permanent, though the exact constellation of forces might change.

The change could, of course, be dramatic and fundamental. Within a declining economy the threat of famine and of general unrest could produce at any time a sudden shift in the balance of forces and even the collapse of the regime. The factional character of Indonesian politics makes for an open and fluid political situation, and despite the President's apparently complete dominance there are groups that could combine to establish an alternative government. The Army has been mentioned. Over against it, and balancing it in a sense, is the Communist Party, which is strong in numbers and in influence. Indeed, to many Western observers the PKI represents the major alternative to the current regime. But its importance must not be overrated. It is true that, in spite of the naturally hostile Moslem environment, it is the largest and best organized Asian Communist party outside China, claiming a membership of about 2.5 million. It is equally true that the strength of the party has developed as a result of the pursuit of moderate policies that have appealed to nationalist rather than to specifically Communist sentiment. Indeed, because of its policies as fashioned under the Aidit leadership, the PKI has placed itself in something of a dilemma. It has played an opportunistic game, gradually repairing its forces, attempting to avoid suppression from above and to capture even Moslem support from below, but it has reached a point from which it would be difficult for it to go further without displaying a militancy that might well lose much of its support and might also invite swift counteraction from the Army. It has suffered from the general constriction of political party activity that has accompanied guided democracy. And it must be remembered that it is essentially a Java-based party which would find it difficult, even if it could seize power at the center, to hold the country as a whole.[3] But it remains a very important element in the power situation. Finally the old oppositionist elements of PSI and Masjumi have survived the banning of the political parties through which they formerly expressed themselves. And individual leaders, including some within the government

[3] For a discussion of this dilemma, see Donald Hindley, "The PKI and the Peasants," *Problems of Communism*, Vol. XI, No. 6 (November-December 1962).

itself, have their own independent following. Chairul Saleh,[4] to mention one, has emerged as a figure of some moment who could no doubt turn a critical situation to his own advantage.

But this is to speculate. In the meantime it may be said that Presidential power has depended, in effect, upon the delicacy of the balance which has existed, and in a sense it might be argued that Sukarno's achievement has been the preservation of stability in a very unstable situation.

Forms and Symbols

Within this style of political framework, what has been the character of government actions and policies? Clearly, the record of guided democracy has not been a happy one. The political changes of 1959 and after have not arrested economic decline. Staple exports have fallen, foreign reserves have been depleted, inflation has continued to spiral, and bureaucratic inefficiency and corruption have become routine. But economic crisis has not evoked any clear program of action to remedy it. The diffusion of political power to which we have referred makes positive action difficult, of course— and raises important questions concerning one of Sukarno's leading political principles—that of consensus. The fact that there was no clear center of authority might be held to justify the attempt to secure agreement by deliberation. At the same time it is also a fact that, on many major questions, there is no consensus. Where genuine differences of interest exist, deliberation by itself is not enough to bridge the gap.

It is perhaps because of this that the introduction of guided democracy has been marked by an extraordinary concern with forms and with symbols. The striking thing about Sukarno's intervention from 1957 onward has been the fact that he has shown little sense of policy though much of machinery. His proposed National Council of 1957, based on functional representation, illustrates the style of his approach. He has been concerned with the forms of government

---

[4] Third Deputy Prime Minister (1964) and Minister for Basic Industries. During the revolution he was associated with the followers of the former PKI leader Tan Malaka, and in the later stages of the revolution he opposed all negotiations with the Dutch. He led a West Java People's Brigade, an independent guerrilla force which opposed the Round Table terms. This force was suppressed by the Republic and Chairul Saleh was arrested. After his release by the Wilopo government some years later, he spent several years in Europe, but returned in 1956 and became one of the early supporters of the President's plan for guided democracy.

and not with the substance that might be implemented through the forms. His monument is the cluster of councils he created within the framework of the Constitution of 1945. The Supreme Advisory Council and the People's Deliberative Assembly were of course provided for in the Constitution itself. But the National Planning Council, the National Front, the Body to Develop the Potential of the Functional Groups, and a variety of other bodies were new conceptions. Consistent with the emphasis on forms has been the concern with slogans. The political principles of the republic are summed up in the compound abbreviation Manipol/USDEK. The President's speech of August 17, 1959, has become known as the political manifesto of the Republic, abbreviated to Manipol, while the initial letters of the five points—the Constitution of 1945, Indonesian socialism, guided democracy, guided economy, and Indonesian "identity"—form the term USDEK. These have become the shibboleths of public political discourse. The ideas they express are too vague to offer any guide to action, but respectful reference to them has become obligatory, a required ritual, a test of trustworthiness. At times the pursuit of forms can reach absurd lengths as when the paragraphs, sections, and parts of the Eight-Year Plan were numbered to reflect the date of independence—17/8/1945. It is in this world of symbol manipulation that one finds the most suggestive evidence of a genuine decline in liberality as guided democracy replaced ordinary democracy. For all that has been said of the limits that still surround Presidential and Army power and of the balance between the two, and for all the theories of deliberation and consensus, there has emerged a sense of orthodoxy that was absent before.

The informal pressures of orthodoxy have been reinforced by more direct controls. Supervision of the press has been close and rigorous, and those newspapers that have published anything remotely resembling criticism of the government have been suppressed. The educational system has become an important instrument for inculcating an acceptance of the official ideology. More drastic action has been taken against individual opponents of the regime. Whereas in the past political heretics could be tolerated, there have been enough arrests to demonstrate clearly that, in the new environment, heresy is dangerous. Finally, the changing character of the bureaucracy itself has revealed new methods of control. Competition for position within the civil service is far more open than it was in the early days of the Republic when the experiment in liberal democracy was accompanied by the creation of recognized institutional controls within the bureaucracy. The decline in respect for rules and regular procedures in political life has had its counterpart in the decay of institutionalized procedures for advancement in the service. Patronage is more important and so is the application of tests of loyalty rather than competence to officials. "Retooling"—the process of replacing the less loyal by the more loyal—is the regular technique for securing a subservient service.

Where so much of the effort of the national leadership has been concerned with bolstering the authority of the regime, and propagating appropriate images of national solidarity and revolutionary purpose, it is not surprising that little progress has been made in grappling with genuine problems of economic development. Indeed the integrative tasks, because of their costliness and their disturbance of proper priorities, have militated against the performance of developmental tasks. The rapidity of inflation bears witness to the seriousness of the economic crisis, though Indonesia's agrarian economy has been able to show greater resilience in the face of the crisis than many observers considered possible some years ago. The take-over of Dutch enterprises in 1957 brought additional administrative problems in its train, and though socialism has been an avowed long-term goal of all governments, the sudden extension of the government-owned sector of the economy preceded the development of the appropriate skills to handle it. Excessive regulation and red tape have made for inefficiency and encouraged corruption. In 1963 the President's Economic Declaration (Dekon) and the Regulations of May 26 that followed it gave promise of a more rigorous approach to economic problems, but the initial drive was hampered by Indonesia's increasingly adventurist foreign policy, by left-wing opposition, by sheer inertia, and by the death in 1963 of the one man—Prime Minister Djuanda—who might have attempted to carry the plan through.

The agitational character of domestic politics has had its counterpart in external policy. At the beginning of her existence as an independent republic, Indonesia adopted a neutralist position, but the character of her neutralism has changed as the balance of her internal political life altered. Neutralism can take many forms. In the early 1950s Indonesia was neutralist with a slight inclination toward the West. By 1960, partly because the failure to acquire West

Irian had sharpened the stridency of her nationalism, partly because of the importance of arms from the Soviet Union and the Communist bloc, partly perhaps because of domestic political developments, her inclination was in the opposite direction. But while this is admitted, it must be firmly stressed that the change did not represent any commitment on Indonesia's part, nor was it, as some Western observers have argued, the result of the improved internal position of the PKI.

During this period the West New Guinea question was the dominating issue of foreign policy. This question was left unresolved at the Round Table Conference in 1949. Five years later, still unresolved, it reached the agenda of the United Nations. In 1957 Indonesia's mounting campaign expressed itself in the expropriation of Dutch property. The 1958 revolt interrupted the campaign temporarily, but its suppression was followed by renewed pressure and by a systematic arms build up, leading finally in 1962 to the agreement whereby the territory was to pass into Indonesia's hands after a brief period of formal U.N. administration. The principle of self-determination was part of this agreement: Indonesia was to allow the inhabitants of West New Guinea an opportunity to determine their own future by 1969, i.e., only after the territory had been administered for some years by Indonesia.

With the resolution of this question, however, Indonesia did not turn to a concentration upon her domestic problems. Since 1962 she has directed considerable effort to her opposition to the new federation of Malaysia. Though she had tacitly approved—or at least not officially opposed—the plans for the foundation of the federation when they were first mooted she chose officially to support the movement of resistance in Brunei, seeing it as a general movement of resistance in the northern Borneo territories as a whole, and in 1963 she began to define her policy of "confrontation." Oddly enough that policy has not been applied with uniform firmness. Statements of undying hostility to Malaysia have been interspersed with more conciliatory postures. Occasional indications of a willingness to negotiate with the new federation have been followed by demonstrations of renewed hostility. These sudden switches of policy may suggest that Indonesian hostility to Malaysia was less the result of a clear clash of interests than a matter of calculated policy. Such a view certainly fits the character of Indonesian domestic policies as we have described them. The whole attitude to Malaysia may be interpreted as being, in considerable measure, an extension of the agitational style of domestic political behavior. Just as the Asian Games, or monuments, or slogans about continuing revolution have helped to consolidate popular feeling, so external issues also may provide at once a rallying point for national sentiment and a means of diverting attention from possible points of criticism of the regime. West Irian had provided such an issue. Once solved it was necessary to find another. From the point of view of the President, external policy could be used as one means of enabling him to preserve the political initiative in his own hands.

This is not the whole story. It is necessary also to take account of unnecessary provocation from the Malayan side, and to recognize that, as the most powerful nation in the region, Indonesia has felt entitled to some consultation in the disposition of regions which border on her territory. It is important also to understand her natural suspicion of anything that may seem to resemble colonialism, and the character of her view of the outside world. The division of the world into new emerging forces and old established forces is not merely an ideological smoke-screen; it does strike a genuine chord in Indonesian thinking. But the consequence of such a view has undoubtedly been to disturb the international stability of the region of which Indonesia forms a part.

If the forms of guided democracy are not as sinister as some critics of the regime have regarded them it has clearly not achieved, either in domestic or foreign policy, a solution to Indonesia's problems. Any judgment, however, must also notice that those problems are not such as to lend themselves to easy solution, and it is important for a foreign observer to recognize the difficulties posed by rising population pressure, shortage of technicians and administrators, and potential divisions within the Indonesian community. In this situation the integrative role of the President has been an important factor in preserving unity, and his theory of guided democracy has reflected a genuine belief in the importance of harmony and consultation as a basis for political action. At the same time it is clear that its achievements have fallen far short of its goals.

Diversity and the Struggle for Power

The way in which these developments may best be interpreted

remains a matter for exploration and debate. Where should the proper emphasis be placed in ordering the multiplicity of events which go to make up the story of Indonesian independence? Which factors, if any, may be regarded as dominant? What models of political behavior can best illuminate a very complex situation? And how far back into Indonesia's past does one need to look in order to understand her present?

In some respects Indonesia's political problem was one shared with other newly emergent states in Africa and Asia. She was confronted with the necessity of constructing a modern state upon a pre-industrial social structure that had been conditioned and distorted by the pressures of a colonial regime. The narrowness of her Western-educated elite and the gap between it and the mass of the agrarian population was in any case not likely to favor the operation of a borrowed democratic system. The gap between elite and mass is blurred, of course, and rapid social change has altered its outlines even since 1949. The extension of education, the enormous growth in the number of white-collar workers, the magnitude of urban growth, increases in newspaper and magazine circulation, and in political party activity even at the village level, have all contributed to the further disruption of agrarian society which had been shaken severely by war, occupation, and revolution. However the life of approximately 80 per cent of the population continues to be ordered within the confines of village society, and requires the maintenance of appropriate forms of administration.

In this situation, though political parties sought to develop a basis of mass support among the agricultural population, effective political action was confined to the ranks of the elite, to the extent almost of displaying an ingrown character. Within the political world of Djakarta the political game was an intimate affair in which party leaders, parliamentarians, or bureaucrats possessed close personal knowledge of each other, and shared a long experience of common political activity. Small as this elite was, it was in no sense monolithic. Its character and composition had been the product of half a century's transformation of Indonesian society. Long before the revolution, the patterns of a traditional order were in process of erosion. Status had long ceased to be determined by birth; though birth remained an important factor, official position, professional skill, or political record had become as important. After 1949 the pattern of overlapping status systems became still more complex, and this had its impact upon the conflict for power.[5] Some of the divisions within the elite have been sketched in broad outline in an earlier chapter: the divisions between older aristocracy and new men, between those who had devoted themselves to political activism and those who were concerned to preserve a smoothly operating governmental machine, between parties, particularly between those seeking an Islamic state and those opposing it in the name of the Pantja Sila, between bureaucratic factions of different party affiliations, and between rival segments of the Army (for instance, the upholders of revolutionary traditions versus the exponents of greater professionalization). These all contributed to the complexity of intra-elite competition.

Cutting across these divisions at some points, reinforcing them at others, was the geographical disunity of the country, the existence of strong regional feeling and the problem of ethnic rivalries. Indonesia's regional problem is not easy to define since it is compounded of a number of elements, not all of which are strictly "regional" in character.[6] The factor of ethnic loyalty is of obvious importance. In the case of large and self-conscious communities such as the Minangkabau, there is to be found a strong pride in the distinctness of their cultural tradition, of their social organization, and of their language, which takes precedence over feelings of national loyalty in certain situations. In some cases religious distinctness accentuates the feeling of identity of a particular community—Protestant Christianity among the Toba Bataks or in Minahasa, the particular strength of Islam in Atjeh or western Sumatra or southern Celebes.

Ethnic relations are complicated by the uneven distribution of population throughout the islands. The fact that approximately 60 per cent of the population of Indonesia lives on the island of Java, combined with the fact that the outer islands are the main producers of Indonesia's exports (about half of the country's exports go out through the two Sumatran ports of Palembang and Belawan) give rise to the feeling that the island of Java, as a net consumer, is a parasite upon the economic energies of the outer islands. The outer islands produce foreign exchange, it is argued, and in return

---

[5] Leslie H. Palmier, *Social Status and Power in Java* (London, 1960) gives an account of overlapping systems of status within a Javanese town. Aristocratic origins, commerce, government service, and eminence in the world of Islam were all competing constituents of prestige and power.

[6] For some discussion of the nature of regional feeling, see J. D. Legge, *Central Authority and Regional Autonomy in Indonesia, 1950-1960* (Ithaca, N.Y., 1961).

they receive less than their fair share of government services and of imported capital goods purchased on the basis of their export earnings. Foreign exchange control has tended to discriminate against producers rather than consumers, and the resentment at this fact has taken on a regionalist coloring. The outer island hostility to Java is, however, directed particularly toward the ethnic Javanese.[7] The Javanese are Indonesia's largest single ethnic group and form approximately half of the total population of the country. Both under the Dutch and since they have been associated with government and administration, and their social ethic has reflected the bureaucratic cast of their own society, making them unsympathetic toward the commercial outlook of entrepreneurs in the outer islands. Many in the outer islands resent what they regard as the undue predominance of Javanese in government service in the country as a whole, and some describe it as constituting Javanese imperialism. These elements of regional and ethnic feeling contributed, as we have seen, to the sharpness of party rivalries in the years when parties represented an important route to power through the parliamentary system. Reference has already been made to the strength of Masjumi in western Sumatra and in southern Sulawesi and also, in western Java, and to the way in which regional feeling and party rivalry thus helped to reinforce each other.

Ethnic and regional diversity served as an argument for the Dutch attempt to establish a federal structure of government for Indonesia. The federal plan, however, was viewed by nationalist leaders as a Dutch-inspired move to weaken the Republic, and though the Round Table Agreement of 1949 had set up a United States of Indonesia, this was converted to a unitary republic within a year, with the almost complete unanimity of the federal parliament. Even so, federal sentiment did continue to exist, and efforts made to counter it by the concession of a large measure of autonomy to regional governments were largely unsuccessful. A radical local government law of 1957 was not sufficient to allay regional suspicion of Djakarta, and in fact its implementation was interrupted by the actual outbreak of regional revolt.

The complaints of the regions were only in part concerned with the desire to run their own affairs. The question was complicated and reinforced by a host of other elements—the conflicting interests of

[7] It is important to distinguish the Javanese, to be found in the central and eastern part of the island of Java, from the Sundanese, whose home is the western third of the island

producer groups as against consumers, of Masjumi versus PNI, of entrepreneurs versus bureaucrats, of divisions within the Army where local commanders were involved with the leadership of the rebellion. None of these antitheses is complete. But in 1958 a number of broad oppositions within the country—sectional, regional, ethnic—ran together and crystallized the challenge of revolt against the center. The defeat of the revolt removed certain important interests from any share in political power, it dramatically changed the balance of forces within Indonesia and it clarified political alignments for the next few years.

Thus various types of division formed the general environment for the struggle for influence and power in the first decade of independent Indonesia's existence. The small number of the politically articulate, the disunity that existed within that small number, the ethnic and regionalist complications combined to contribute to the fact that Indonesia lacked a strong focus of power. That fact in itself perhaps enabled the forms of liberal democracy to function for a time. The absence of a concentration of power rendered any other alternative out of the question. But it impeded the exercise of adequately firm authority, and lack of such authority contributed to men's willingness to see liberal democratic institutions overthrown. The open rivalry of the early years was eventually to lead to a consolidation of power, not into the hands of one man or one group, but at least into fewer and more clearly defined centers.

Keys to Contemporary Indonesia

Attempts have been made to define the basic, underlying factors in this complex situation. One of the most illuminating analyses of Indonesian politics has based itself on the concept of a growing tension between two clearly distinguishable types of leadership to be observed within the elite. On the one hand are those who have been concerned to grapple in unexciting fashion with specific economic and administrative problems, to negotiate and apply practical solutions to limited questions. On the other hand are those who have devoted themselves to integrative tasks: to the consolidation of national feeling, the manipulation of mass movements, the elaboration of national ideology, the fashioning of a spectacular foreign policy. The members of the former group have been termed "administrators" and the members of the latter "solidarity makers." The distinction between the two types of leader, and between the skills displayed by each, forms the core of the argument of Feith's account of the decline of constitutional democracy during the period of independence.[8] The administrators possessed "administrative, technical, legal, and foreign-language skills required to run the distinctively modern apparatus of a modern state." The solidarity makers were "skilled as mediators between groups at different levels of modernity and political effectiveness, as mass organizers, and as manipulators of integrative symbols." [9] The distinction flowed across party lines and functional divisions. Individual party leaders might be sober problem-solvers. Individual bureaucrats might be well endowed with manipulative skills. Military leaders might display either type of talent. In Feith's account the administrators find their supreme example in the person of Hatta, but such other leaders of the early republic as Natsir, Sukiman, and Wilopo also fall into that category. The most obvious representative of the solidarity maker group is the President himself.

During the revolution both types of skill had been necessary, and they were equally necessary for the task of nation building after independence. Problem solving and the maintenance of general support for the new regime were complementary to each other. But advocating contrasting approaches to national leadership, the two groups tended to see each other as enemies, and so there was conflict between them, a conflict that was manifest within a number of the government parties, between several cabinets and their opposition and between factional groups in the Army. In the absence of other centers of power in the country, of opposing classes or other organized interests to which individuals or factions might be firmly anchored, politics had a cliquist character. As Feith puts it, "the principal unit of political competition was the virtually free-floating clique, an informal group of leaders with personal followings and personal ties to one another." [10] And one important determinant of the lines of clique cleavage was the type of skills that a particular group of leaders had and upon which they could stake claims to power and office.

The two groups in fact represented fundamentally different types of person. The members of the administrator skill group, secure in their technical competence, tended to underestimate the need to win political support for government policies. Good government seen in predominantly economic and administrative terms seemed to them to be sufficient legitimation in itself. Most of the members of this

[8] *The Decline of Constitutional Democracy in Indonesia* (Ithaca, 1962).
[9] *Ibid.*, p. 113.
[10] *Ibid.*, p. 115

group had enjoyed a Western higher education and had succeeded in making a satisfactory accommodation with the modern world. Their outlook comprised indigenous elements as well as Western ones, but at least it offered a coherent enough system of values and included the idea of the pursuit of political goals through established rules and procedures. Members of the solidarity maker group by contrast tended to be men whose pride lay in the fact that they, unlike the administrators, were "close to the people." In effect they spoke particularly for uprooted people, persons who had lost their old values as a result of social and political upheaval and not found security in an alternative set of values. For these, political activity was not a means of pursuing clearly defined goals. It tended rather to be an end in itself. Usually poorly educated, such people lacked a sense of acknowledged technical capacity to sustain them. For a time the revolutionary struggle had made their lives meaningful, but their sense of meaning did not carry over into the humdrum years of peace. So they tended to be attracted by leaders offering to make government and politics meaningful again, and hence to respond to messianic and agitational appeals of many kinds. These people, in Feith's term, formed the "constituency" of the solidarity makers.[11]

On the basis of this distinction, Feith proceeds to interpret the failure of the experiment in liberal democracy in terms of the declining influence of administrators and the gradual, though never entirely complete, victory of solidarity makers. He argues that constitutionalism was instituted by the administrators as a system that could serve their interests, inasmuch as they feared chaos and mob rule and wanted politics to operate through established rules and procedures. They adopted the system when their power was at its zenith and operated it with some success in succeeding years. During this period they addressed themselves with not inconsiderable success to practical problems. But they failed to build themselves support among the uprooted of the revolutionary generation, and so they enjoyed little popularity. By the end of 1952 they had lost their previous position of hegemony within the Army, and the following year saw the formation of the first of a series of cabinets dominated by their rivals, the solidarity makers. Thenceforth the emphasis of cabinets was less on practical administrative and economic problems and more on foreign policy and agitational campaigns to demonstrate popular support for the struggle for West Irian. After 1958, when President Sukarno

[11] *Ibid.*, p. 119.

reached his position of great personal power, these concerns were sup-
plemented by a concentration on the development of ideology, on
spectacular demonstrations of national prestige, and on the building
up of military strength at great cost to the national economy. In
devoting themselves to the ceremonial aspects of politics and to the
search for an ideal image that could give meaning to political activity
and to life in general, the solidarity makers, under Sukarno's leadership, were less and less concerned with economic realities. Manipol/
USDEK, the idea of continuing revolution, the Asian Games and the
Games of the New Emerging Forces, the struggle for West Irian and
the confrontation with Malaysia, the overseas trips for the President,
the rebuilding of Djakarta and the erection of imposing monuments
—all these took precedence over urgent economic problems, particularly after the dismantling of the parliamentary system and the rule-
based style of political behavior which had been a basic aspect of that
system.

The process had its own built-in momentum. Since competition for
patronage, place, and power was very much on the basis of contrasting
skills, those who could advance themselves through their capacity for
political action have felt themselves constantly threatened by others
who possessed a greater claim by virtue of their technical knowledge
and administrative capacity. Hence they have been compelled to
justify their tenure of office by loyalty and enthusiasm, by their adherence to ideological themes, by the use of slogans, and by the
manipulation of symbols. In accepting and propagating the image of
a powerful Indonesia, they were not merely exercising their skills; they
were also engaged in defense against rivals. The rules and procedures
of parliamentary democracy were thus discarded, for their function
had been to protect "the technician against the leader, the competent
man against the man with the right spirit, the man who can do a particular job well against the man who can give meaning and purpose
to the totality of jobs." [12]

In developing his administrator–solidarity maker dichotomy, Feith
is frankly concerned to portray ideal types, to present a model of political behavior that can be used to illuminate important interconnec-
tions in the real world. His distinction is not intended to be a clear
and absolute one, and reality can offer many exceptions. There are
leaders who combine both types of skill, and others who fit easily into

[12] Feith, "The Dynamics of Guided Democracy," in Ruth T. McVey, ed.,
Indonesia (New Haven, 1963), p. 389.

neither category. Insofar as the distinction is useful, it might be argued that a similar distinction may be observed in other societies. But for all this, the model does have an obviously high correspondence with the reality of contemporary Indonesia, and it does draw attention to characteristics of the political scene which may have echoes elsewhere, but which exist here in striking form. Like all good analytical devices, Feith's distinction, once formulated, strikes the observer with the blinding force of the obvious, and succeeds in throwing light on many aspects of the political scene.

Any such analysis has its limitations, of course. It can offer only a part of the story. To criticize it within its own terms of reference, it may be argued that to focus the spotlight on competitive leadership skills could lead to a preoccupation with the mechanics of political behavior rather than with its underlying causes. We are told a great deal about how the two skill groups behave but not so much about who composes them—except of course in terms of the skills themselves and the level of training and the individual dispositions that produced them. This may be the fault of the subject matter. It may not be possible in Indonesia to link either of Feith's skill groups with any clearly identifiable class or interest in the community. His idea of the solidarity maker's "constituency" is itself a recognition of the difficulty. Being an administrator or a solidarity maker, in short, cannot be correlated with other categories, with economic position, for example, or ethnic origin, but really only with education on the one hand and rootlessness on the other. Hence the concept of "free-floating" cliques, groups that by definition cannot be identified by criteria other than their adherence to a particular leader. Cliquism of this kind undoubtedly forms a very significant element in the mechanics of Indonesian politics. But it is important that an attempt be made to consider what features of Indonesian society and of the Indonesian outlook encourage a cliquist style of political behavior or promote a solidarity maker victory over the administrator. Is there, for example, anything particularly Indonesian in the concern with the form and ritual rather than with the substance of politics? If so, has this any connection with the contemplative approach to life displayed by the Javanese aristocracy, or with the agrarian character of Indonesian society, or with other aspects of her history?

Feith hints at a way of escape from too mechanistic a view of politics by setting his administrator-solidarity maker antithesis within the broader concept of his two dominant political cultures—the Javanese aristocratic and the Islamic entrepreneurial—a contrast that draws attention to Indonesia's geographical and ethnic divisions and to special aspects of her historical development. And indeed the fact of increasingly acrimonious relations between representatives of these two political cultures forms a central part of his explanation of why constitutional democracy was overthrown and abandoned. But, perhaps inevitably, this is linked only loosely with his identification of the two opposing skill groups. He tells us relatively little, for example, about why it is among the Javanese that the solidarity makers have had their easiest successes.

It is instructive to compare Feith's approach with a quite different attempt at an interpretation of the events of the past decade—an interpretation which finds its central theme in the field of interethnic conflict. Such an approach is developed by Leslie H. Palmier in the course of a consideration of Indonesia's relations with the Netherlands.[13]

Palmier, in addressing himself to the problem of the increasing intransigence displayed by both sides after 1950, is drawn into a consideration of Indonesia's domestic politics, and he concludes unequivocally that at the root of Indonesian xenophobia, and also of the unstable character of internal politics, lies "a fundamental conflict between the Javanese and the non-Javanese." [14]

In the early stages of his argument, Palmier draws attention to the consequences of the multi-party system with which Indonesia began her democratic experiment (and to the parallel consequences of the Netherlands' multi-party system of rule). In a two-party system either party can afford to ignore its extremists and, in competing for the popular vote, is in fact forced to bid for moderate support. The electoral system thus reduces the intensity of political disagreement and leads the two contenders to gravitate toward the center. By contrast, in a multi-party system based on proportional representation, even small parties have a chance of survival, and will therefore tend to seek support by asserting their distinctiveness and emphasizing even those minor differences that mark them off from their rivals. Extremist attitudes are encouraged and moderation is at a discount. In the situation under discussion, argues Palmier, both Indonesia and the Netherlands were persuaded, by the mechanism of their representative systems, to adopt unyielding attitudes to each other. But in the more important

---

[13] Leslie H. Palmier, *Indonesia and the Dutch* (London, 1962).
[14] *Ibid.* p. 170.

part of his argument, Palmier goes on to draw attention to the part played by kinship, and therefore by ethnic origin, in providing a binding force for the principal parties in Indonesia.[15] He stresses (with appropriate qualifications) the facts we have already noted—the strength of PNI, NU, and PKI in central and eastern Java, and the weakness of Masjumi in that area. He refers to Javanese dominance in the civil service[16] and to the operation of the Constitution of the unitary state (1950), which naturally gave greater representation to greater numbers and so favored the Javanese. The PNI–Masjumi rivalry of 1950-56 may seem to have been based on differences of program—the difference between attitudes to economic development, for example, when Masjumi was ready to accept foreign capital while PNI and the other Javanese parties looked to "Indonesianization" and revealed what might be called a bureaucratic rather than an entrepreneurial approach to the problem. In essence, however, these differences of program were really, he believes, the accompaniments of a more general ethnic opposition. Javanese aristocratic social structures were inimical to commercial activity, but in the outer islands, trade was "a natural way of life." [17] Finally, Palmier sees the collapse of constitutionalism and the trend toward guided democracy as reflecting the further dominance of "the Javanese faction," operating now not through parties but in other ways.

The elections of 1955 had strengthened the position of the Java-based parties, PNI, NU, and PKI. Whereas in the provisional parliament they had held 73 out of 233 seats, the elections gave them 149 seats out of a total of 257.[18] This new distribution reduced the need for a Javanese compromise with the non-Javanese. The change in the balance of power received symbolic expression with the resignation of Hatta as Vice-President in December 1956, and the breaking of his long-established cooperation with Sukarno. The non-Javanese therefore turned to other means of asserting their influence. The attempted coup of November 1956, when the Sumatran Colonel Zulkifli Lubis attempted to seize control of Djakarta, is seen as a non-Javanese move against a Javanese-dominated central government. The subsequent moves by provincial military commanders in Sumatra and Celebes, and the revolt of 1958, are seen in similar terms. The defeat of the

[15] *Ibid.*, p. 151-52.
[16] *Ibid.*, p. 154.
[17] *Ibid.*, p. 155.
[18] *Ibid.*, p. 160.

revolt and the later banning of Masjumi confirmed Javanese dominance. Throughout the whole period Sukarno himself is described as having "unmistakably identified himself with the Javanese faction, especially the PNI and the Communists," [19] and the assertion of his direct political intervention, beginning with the establishment of his National Council in 1957, reaching its climax with the adoption by Presidential decree of the Constitution of 1945, represented the means by which Javanese authority was exercised.

Palmier's analysis of events has the appeal of clarity and simplicity, and it does seek to provide the sort of unifying explanation that Feith avoids. The attempt is not entirely successful, however. Reality is rarely simple and clear, and if Feith is a little hesitant in his search for underlying historical causes, Palmier places too much weight upon one single factor. The fundamental differences of attitude and outlook between Javanese and other groups to which he draws attention are certainly deeply rooted in Indonesian history. But he makes too rigid a contrast between the Javanese and the rest. His account needs to be qualified by a recognition of non-ethnic elements and of other factors that cut across the lines of ethnic division. The plan for the extension of regional autonomy, to take one central example, does not fit the ethnic analysis. It must be noticed that regional disaffections reached their climax after the central government had made a genuine effort to concede extensive powers of regional autonomy. Those concessions were made under a Javanese Minister who found himself at odds with his Department on the question. The subsequent withdrawal of the concessions was effected under a Sundanese minister. There were ethnic elements present in regional demands for greater freedom from central control, but the story cannot be told solely or even mainly in those terms.[20]

The difficulty of finding a neat interpretation that can draw diverse forces into a coherent whole brings us back to a central characteristic of the Indonesian scene—the fact that political conflicts have been very much a matter of a game at the top, of rivalries within an elite. It is this fact that accounts for Feith's inability to tie his leadership categories to social classes, and for the unsatisfactory character of Palmier's analysis in ethnic terms. Nevertheless, it is possible to discern at least some alignments based on class or regional or religious

[19] *Ibid.*, p. 153.
[20] See Legge, *op. cit.*, for a discussion of the local government experiment.

or ethnic differences, and the story we have outlined of the President holding in balance a diversity of pressures, cannot be told purely in terms of cliques competing for power. As we have suggested, Feith's concept of a variety of political cultures is useful here, and it has its advantages over the Palmier analysis. In drawing attention to a number of such political cultures of which the Javanese-aristocratic and the Islamic-entrepreneurial cultures are dominant, it avoids a single all-embracing dichotomy. In consequence, it allows scope for the play of other factors that do not fit the ethnic antithesis—Feith's own antithesis of administrator versus solidarity maker, the play of party rivalry in the early years of independence, the organizational skills of the Communist Party, the increasingly important role of a professional Army, the variants within Islam, and, underlying them all, the intransigent problems of population growth, of economic decline, and of popular disillusionment with the fruits of independence, all of which contribute to the growth of an inherently unstable situation. It provides, at the same time, a broad historical perspective which must be remembered when these other factors are under examination.

One further important characteristic of the Indonesian scene has not received the attention it deserves from political analysts—the role of the capital in political life. Djakarta is a phenomenon in itself. It is the center at which the country's political pressures are brought to bear. It is the focal point of intense political activity, of elbowing for position and patronage, and its shadow-world of gossip and intrigue creates a heightened atmosphere within which competing pressures operate. Djakarta contains within it a mosaic of ethnic groups, reproducing in microcosm the rivalries that exist outside it, and the structure of its society too reflects in accentuated form the divisions of the wider Indonesian society. But the struggle for power there sometimes seems to bear only a tenuous relationship to the way in which life goes on in the country at large. There is an artificial element, no doubt, in the atmosphere of all political capitals; but Djakarta politics seem more remote than usual from the society of which they form a part. Impressionistic generalizations aside, there is room for study of the complex pattern of personal relationships with the Djakarta elite, and of the extent to which it is a self-contained elite.

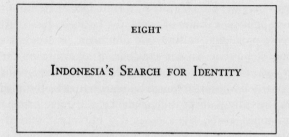

EIGHT

INDONESIA'S SEARCH FOR IDENTITY

It has been possible in these pages to sketch only in broad outline the varied society that Indonesia possesses—with its labor-intensive agriculture, its villages and its peasantry, its traditional aristocracy, the major commerce of its periphery and the minor commerce deep within the interstices of rural life, its mixture of faiths, and—just as much a part of the scene—its educated elite, its new bureaucracy, its intra-elite conflicts, its largely nationalized system of estates, its recently acquired military power. In describing this society, and in attempting to disentangle the elements that make up its complex of cultural traditions, we have returned from time to time, and in different connections, to the themes of continuity and innovation, of tradition versus rapid change, of the interaction between the distant and the more recent past. Is the modern republic the creation of Dutch colonial rule, or do its most important characteristics flow from remoter sources, from Arabia, from India, or from still more ancient origins?

This question has been given point in an odd way in contemporary Indonesia, as the modern republic has become more and more emphatic that its citizens be true to their "Indonesian identity." The current trend is in some ways an unexpected development. President Sukarno's insistence that guided democracy must draw its strength from the deeper values of the Indonesian tradition stands in interesting contrast to the self-conscious rejection of the past that was to be observed in much prewar nationalist thinking. To a great extent, as was suggested at the end of Chapter Six, the contemporary return to tradition is a nativistic movement—an artificial emphasis of so-called traditional values, which, simply because they are emphasized in this way, can no longer be quite what they were. They are called upon to perform a new function in the contemporary situation, and they must therefore be examined in the context of that situation. Just as Shintoism in Japan in the 1930s was an ideological prop for the country's nationalistic self-assertion and not a genuine revival of the beliefs of antiquity, so the application of the principles of deliberation and consensus (*musjawarah* and *mufakat*) to the operations of Indonesian central government must be seen as part of the ideological equipment of the modern Indonesian state. At the same time it is clear to even a superficial glance that in many ways the patterns of the past do lie close to the surface of the present in Indonesia. There is a genuine sense of tradition, which affects the country's approach to the tasks of modern government, and the question of the relative weight to be given to continuity and change does appear to pose a real problem of judgment.

The question of the degree to which a society may change and yet retain its own identity is difficult to answer. In Chapter Two it was suggested that the antithesis that has often been drawn between traditional society and the developments that followed intensive Dutch investment and government is a misleading antithesis, and later chapters have attempted to show that no sharp contrast can be made between the two. In the first place so-called traditional society was itself not a static and unchanging entity. Hindu influences altered the forms of the agrarian order that had emerged by the early centuries of the Christian era, participation in overseas trade brought further changes, and the infiltration of Islam brought its own distinctive contribution. Indonesian society on the eve of European penetration was different in a host of ways from the society that had existed 800 years before. But these developments were gradual—not sudden, catastrophic, and revolutionary. Secondly the effect in the end was to produce not a simple coherent culture, but rather a multiplicity of traditions, many of them retaining vigorous life. There is a variety of threads to be distinguished in the modern pattern, not an even blending of color. Indonesian history has been a triumph of coexistence.

For all this the changes of the later part of the nineteenth century and the early twentieth century fall into a different category from those that preceded them. In the seventeenth and eighteenth centuries the Dutch had begun to assert their claim to the dominant position in the archipelago which had been held by the Javanese in the days of Madjapahit. In the early nineteenth century the process was accelerated. And toward the end of the century the full pressure of Western industrial society made itself felt. Indonesian society under this pressure remained compounded of many elements, but the Dutch added their own contribution, to some extent directly, but also in a thousand indirect ways. The modern observer is struck from time to time by the "Dutchness" of modern Indonesia, revealed sometimes in the institutions of the country—the legal system, for instance, or the way in which local government organization was planned—and sometimes in more tangible if more superficial ways—the architecture of a bourgeois suburbia, perhaps. The mold of the Dutch educational system was of incalculable importance in contributing to the fashioning of the modern Indonesian intellectual. Apart from these specifically Dutch contributions—and more fundamental—were the broad currents of social change that followed the solvent influences of European industrial civilization, and which have already been sufficiently stressed. For all these reasons there are good grounds for seeing 1870 or thereabouts as marking the end of one era and the beginning of a new one. Even so, and in spite of the magnitude of these developments, the very changes that occurred after 1870 were shaped within the confines of a traditional framework, and the resulting society bore the imprint of the distant as well as the immediate past.

These remarks may seem to be striving after an easy middle way in order to avoid an answer to the question that has been posed: on the one hand there is continuity and on the other there is change. The difficulty arises from the framing of the question in general terms, and from the consequent attempt to give a simple and general answer. In fact an answer cannot be given in the abstract; it is more satisfactory to draw attention to particular themes that arise from Indonesia's island and agricultural character and which can be seen to reassert themselves in the contemporary situation. It is still important, for instance, that Javanese society retains strong elements of an aristocratic order, though the emergence of her new elite has produced shifts in status and the overlapping of alternative and sometimes competing systems of status. It is important that aristocracy has been associated with bureaucratic authority and that the pattern of relationships between government and the mass of the population still reveals traces of the older interacting traditions of court and peasantry. It is important that Islam penetrated unevenly into Indonesian

society and that, for the most part, it has found its greatest strongholds outside Java, and that within Java there is a continuing tension
between the devout and the merely nominal Muslim, between *santri*
and *abangan*. It is important that the outer islands still find themselves in broad opposition to the island of Java, though the country
as a whole displays a tighter political unity than ever before. And it
is important to notice characteristic habits of mind in such features
as the desire for harmony in political life or the preoccupation of
many Indonesian intellectuals with concepts and forms rather than
with the substance of politics. But it is important too that Indonesia's
numbers have increased astronomically, that modern commercial cities have grown, that the country has been brought within the orbit
of a world economy.

In facing the problems posed by these more recent developments,
Indonesia has no need of an artificially constructed "personality" on
which to base her policies and her attitudes. Rather her identity in
the future, as in the past, will reveal itself in how those problems are
handled in practice, and it will no doubt be a subtly changing identity.
If she is to be successful she will need more than the values derived
from a past age and very much more than a narrow and stereotyped
version of those values. She will need a ready willingness to meet the
present on its own terms. This involves no loss of identity. The erosion
of some traditional patterns under the impact of Western industrial-
ism was not simply a destructive process: it was as creative as it was
destructive. The ability to accept new influences and to add them to
the existing diversity of elements in her culture lies, perhaps, at the
core of the real Indonesian identity.

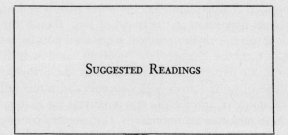

SUGGESTED READINGS

The study of Indonesian society and history by Western scholars has been transformed during the past dozen or so years. Though a small but distinguished group of Dutch scholars has continued to make fundamental contributions, the center of Indonesian studies has shifted decisively during that period from the Netherlands to the United States, from Leiden and Utrecht to American universities and their major area programs and projects. American students have been concerned primarily with problems of the modern republic, as evidenced by the growing body of monographs from, for example, the Cornell Modern Indonesian Project, or M.I.T's Center for International Studies, or Yale's program of Southeast Asia Studies. But this concentration on the present has been accompanied by the elaboration of fresh perspectives on the past as well, carrying forward or complementing the work of earlier or contemporary Dutch students. At the same time the American interest has encouraged the republication in English of seminal works by Dutch writers in the series *Selected Studies on Indonesia by Dutch Scholars*. Some of the writings of B. J. O. Schrieke published in two volumes under the title *Indonesian Sociological Studies* (The Hague, 1955, and Bandung, 1957) and of J. C. van Leur published as *Indonesian Trade and Society* (The Hague and Bandung, 1955) are notable examples. British scholars have also made their contribution over the years. These developments have combined to make available for English-speaking students an extensive body of material. The present work is directed to such students, and this bibliography therefore draws attention principally to works available in English. For the vast body of material available in Dutch, readers should see W. Ph. Coolhaas, *A Critical Survey of Studies on Dutch Colonial History* ('s-Gravenhage, 1960).

Introductory Works

The best analytical introduction to Indonesian history and contemporary society is undoubtedly W. F. Wertheim's *Indonesian Society in Tran-*

sition (The Hague and Bandung, 1956, 2nd revised edition, 1959).
Though first published in the mid-1950s, its perceptive and many-sided
analysis of Indonesian society has not been dated by later developments.
The most readable chronological survey of Indonesian history is still
B. H. M. Vlekke, *Nusantara* (Cambridge, Mass., 1943; revised edition,
The Hague and Bandung, 1959). The revised edition takes account of recent research, and the earlier chapters in particular have been written in a
more tentative vein in the light of C. C. Berg's reinterpretation of the
evidence. The Indonesian sections of D. G. E. Hall, A *History of South-
East Asia* (London, 1955; revised edition, 1964) offer a general text that
also embodies the results of recent scholarship. A shorter text for the general reader is Brian Harrison, *South-East Asia* (London, 1954).

For a deeper introductory treatment of the contemporary scene, see the
sections on Indonesia by George McT. Kahin in Kahin, ed., *Major Governments of Asia* (revised edition, Ithaca, 1963) and by Herbert Feith
in Kahin, ed., *Governments and Politics of Southeast Asia* (revised edition, Ithaca, 1964).

For introductory treatment in more popular form, see Dorothy Wood-
man, *The Republic of Indonesia* (London, 1955), Willard A. Hanna,
Bung Karno's Indonesia (New York, 1961), Louis Fischer, *The Story
of Indonesia* (New York, 1959), and Bruce Grant, *Indonesia* (Mel-
bourne, 1964).

Early History and Hindu Influence

Recent decades have seen important reassessments of the role of Indian
influence in Indonesia and of the character of Indonesian history during
that period of influence. The tradition of Hindu-Javanese studies represented in N. J. Krom's attempt to piece together an acceptable chronological account as represented in his *Hindoe-Javaansche Geschiedenis* (The
Hague, 1931) has been replaced by two approaches: (1) the new criticism
of C. C. Berg, to which brief reference is made in the text, and (2) the
application of general sociological principles to an analysis of available
evidence, notably in B. J. O. Schrieke's studies of the general character of
the Javanese kingdom, "Ruler and Realm in Early Java," published in
English together with other of his writings as *Indonesian Sociological
Studies* (The Hague and Bandung, Vol. I, 1955; Vol. II, 1957); and in
J. C. van Leur's use of Weberian sociology in his essay "On Early Asian
Trade" (*loc. cit.*).

Robert Heine-Geldern, "Conceptions of State and Kingship in South-
East Asia," *Far Eastern Quarterly*, Vol. II, No. 1 (November 1942),
gives an important treatment of patterns of thought and belief. See also
Cora du Bois, *Social Forces in Southeast Asia* (Minnesota, 1949). The
character and extent of Indian influence is considered in H. G. Quaritch
Wales, *The Making of Greater India* (London, 1952), and its method in
F. D. K. Bosch, "The Problem of the Hindu Colonisation of Indonesia"
in his *Selected Studies in Indonesian Archaeology* (The Hague, 1961).
Georges Coedès, *Les États hindouisés d'Indochine et d'Indonésie* (Paris,
1948) is a basic work for the study of the period. For a full bibliographical
note on the period, see J. G. de Casparis, "Historical Writing on Indo-

nesia (Early Period)" in D. G. E. Hall, ed., *Historians of South-East Asia* (London, 1961).

Islamic Influence

For introductory study, the history of Islam in Indonesia is less available than the history of Hindu influence. Some of the works of the great Dutch Islamologist, Christiaan Snouck Hurgronje, are available in English, notably *The Achehnese* (translated by A. W. S. O'Sullivan, Leiden, 1906, 2 vols.). G. W. J. Drewes, "Indonesia: Mysticism and Activism," in G. E. von Grunebaum, ed., *Unity and Variety in Muslim Civilization* (Chicago, 1955) and P. A. Hoesein Djajadiningrat, "Islam in Indonesia," in Kenneth W. Morgan, ed., *Islam—The Straight Path* (New York, 1958) give useful introductory treatment. The best general introductory survey of the history of Islam in Indonesia is to be found in the first three chapters of Harry J. Benda, *The Crescent and the Rising Sun: Indonesian Islam under the Japanese Occupation, 1942-1945* (The Hague and Bandung, 1958).

A. H. Johns, "Sufism as a Category in Indonesian Literature and History," *Journal Southeast Asian History*, Vol. 2, No. 2 (July 1961) discusses the problem of Indonesia's receptivity to a particular variant of Islam. See also B. J. O. Schrieke, "The Shifts in Political and Economic Power in the Indonesian Archipelago in the Sixteenth and Seventeenth Century," in *Indonesian Sociological Studies*, I., and Benda's "Christiaan Snouck Hurgronje and the Foundations of Dutch Islamic Policy in Indonesia," *The Journal of Modern History*, XXX (1958). C. A. O. van Nieuwenhuijze, *Aspects of Islam in Post-Colonial Indonesia* (The Hague and Bandung, 1958) is a series of essays by an Islamic expert of the former Netherlands Indian government. For a sensitive appreciation of the character of modern Indonesian Islam, see Clifford Geertz, *The Religion of Java* (Illinois, 1960).

The Early Colonial Period

This period has not been the subject of recent close analysis. A general treatment is available in D. G. E. Hall's *History of South-East Asia*, and also in J. S. Furnivall's *Netherlands India* (Cambridge, 1939). Van Leur's contribution to the study of commercial patterns has been of crucial importance in revising perspectives concerning the role of the Dutch East Indian Company.

For a close examination of the implications of his argument see John Smail "On the Possibility of an Autonomous History of Modern Southeast Asia," *Journal Southeast Asian History*, Vol. 2, No. 2 (July 1961). See also John Bastin, *The Western Element in Modern Southeast Asian History* (Kuala Lumpur, 1960). For a detailed study of Indonesia's part in Asian trade in the sixteenth and early seventeenth centuries see M. A. P. Meilink-Roelofsz, *Asian Trade and European Influence in the Indonesian Archipelago between 1500 and about 1630* (The Hague, 1962), a work based partly on Portuguese sources not used by van Leur and which revises his thesis in some respects and supports it in others. For a commentary on Meilink-Roelofsz's argument, see D. K. Bassett, European Influence in South-East Asia, c. 1500-1630," *Journal Southeast Asian History*, Vol. 4, No. 2 (September 1963). For a close study of the Dutch East India Company's trade, see Kristof Glamann, *Dutch-Asiatic Trade, 1620-1740* (Copenhagen and The Hague, 1958). George Masselman, *The Cradle of Colonialism* (New Haven and London, 1963) offers an extremely readable account, couched in somewhat heroic terms, of the formation of the East India Company and of the career of Jan Pieterszoon Coen.

Clifford Geertz, *Agricultural Involution: The Process of Ecological Change in Indonesia* (Berkeley and Los Angeles, 1963) includes the most illuminating recent study of the character of the Culture System. See also R. van Niel, "The Function of Landrent under the Cultivation System in Java," *The Journal of Asian Studies*, Vol. XXIII, No. 3 (May 1964).

The Later Colonial Period

J. S. Furnivall, *Netherlands India*, gives a survey and analysis of Dutch policy and its consequences, and his *Colonial Policy and Practice* (Cambridge, 1948) compares British policy in Burma and Dutch policy in the Indies. Amry Vandenbosch, *The Dutch East Indies* (Berkeley and Los Angeles, 1941) is another good general survey. An important if somewhat theoretical Dutch study is A. D. A. De Kat Angelino, *Colonial Policy*, 2 vols. (trans. G. J. Renier, The Hague, 1931). A more recent survey of the whole colonial period is J. J. van Klaveren, *The Dutch Colonial System in the East Indies* (Rotterdam, 1953). For a Dutch apologia see the symposium *Mission Interrupted*, edited by W. H. van Helsdingen and H. Hoogenberk (Amsterdam, 1945).

For a treatment of economic developments, see G. C. Allen and Audrey G. Donnithorne, *Western Enterprise in Indonesia and Malaya* (London, 1957). The "dual economy" theory of J. H. Boeke will be found expounded and criticized in the anthology of writings by Dutch economists, *Indonesian Economics: The Concept of Dualism in Theory and Policy* (The Hague, 1961, published as Vol. VI of *Selected Studies of Indonesia by Dutch Scholars*), and also in Boeke's *The Structure of Netherlands Indian Economy* (New York, 1942), which is a translation of part of an earlier study. Benjamin Higgins, "The Dualistic Theory of Underdeveloped Areas," *Ekonomi dan Keuangan Indonesia* (February 1955; reprinted in *Economic Development and Cultural Change*, Vol. 4, 1956), offers a more recent and more trenchant criticism. Clifford Geertz, *Agricultural Involution*, does something toward reinstating the theory in a new form. See also Manning Nash, "Southeast Asian Society: Dual or Multiple," and Benjamin Higgins, "Comments," in *The Journal of Asian Studies*, Vol. XXIII, No. 3 (May 1964).

A useful study of the Ethical Policy and some of its social and political consequences is provided by R. van Niel, *The Emergence of the Modern Indonesian Elite* (The Hague and Bandung, 1960).

Revolution and Independence

The classical study of the rise of the nationalist movement and of the revolution is George McT. Kahin, *Nationalism and Revolution in Indonesia* (Ithaca, 1952). Harry J. Benda, *The Crescent and the Rising Sun* provides an account of Islam under the Japanese occupation. An account of the role of the United Nations in the struggle for independence is given by Alastair M. Taylor, *Independence and the United Nations* (London, 1960).

Of vital importance as one example of the attitudes of Indonesian intellectual nationalist leaders is Soetan Sjahrir, *Out of Exile* (New York, 1949)—a collection of letters written from exile in New Guinea.

For the history of Indonesian independence, the wealth of studies available makes selection difficult. A large body of monograph material exists —some of it in multilith form, as in the series of Interim Reports and Monographs published by the Cornell Modern Indonesia Project. Herbert Feith, *The Indonesian Elections of 1955* (Ithaca, 1957), A. K. Pringgodigdo, *The Office of President in Indonesia as Defined in the Three Constitutions in Theory and Practice* (Ithaca, 1957), Robert C. Bone, Jr., *The Dynamics of the Western New Guinea (Irian Barat) Problem* (Ithaca, 1958), Harry J. Benda and Ruth T. McVey, *The Communist Uprisings of 1926-1927 in Indonesia: Key Documents* (Ithaca, 1960), Soedjatmoko, *An Approach to Indonesian History: Towards an Open Future* (Ithaca, 1960) are examples. Other works that cover particular aspects are J. H. Brimmell, *Communism in South-East Asia* (London, 1959); Arnold C. Brackman, *Indonesian Communism* (New York, 1963); Donald Hindley, "The PKI and the Peasants," in *Problems of Communism*, Vol. XI, No. 6 (November-December 1962), and his "President Soekarno and the Communists: The Politics of Domestication" in *The American Political Science Review*, Vol. LVI, No. 4 (December 1962); Soedjatmoko, "The Rise of Political Parties in Indonesia," in Phillip W. Thayer, ed., *Nationalism and Progress in Free Asia*; Donald E. Wilmott, *The Chinese in Semarang* (Ithaca, 1961); Leslie H. Palmier, *Indonesia and the Dutch* (London, 1962), and *Social Status and Power in Java* (London, 1960); Selosoemardjan, *Social Changes in Jogjakarta* (Ithaca, 1962); J. D. Legge, *Central Authority and Regional Autonomy in Indonesia, 1950-1960* (Ithaca, 1961); G. William Skinner, ed., *Local Ethnic and National Loyalties in Village Indonesia* (New Haven, 1959).

J. M. van der Kroef, *Indonesia and the Modern World*, 2 vols. (Bandung, 1954 and 1956) contains much interesting material. An excellent recent symposium is Ruth T. McVey, ed., *Indonesia* (New Haven, 1963): Of particular importance in this volume are Herbert Feith's chapter, "The Dynamics of Guided Democracy," and that of Hildred Geertz, "Indonesian Cultures and Communities."

Certain major interpretative contributions do need particular emphasis. The outstanding political history of the first seven years of independence is Herbert Feith, *The Decline of Constitutional Democracy in Indonesia* (Ithaca, 1962). It is important both as an essay in the use of certain analytical techniques and as a penetrating and close study of the course of events. Second, reference should be made to the single-handed achievement of Clifford Geertz in uncovering some of the deeper levels of the Indonesian social and economic order. Aided by his distinguished style, he moves easily across the borders that often separate anthropology, sociology, politics, and economic history. His three early working papers, *The Development of the Javanese Economy: A Socio-Cultural Approach* (Cambridge, Mass., 1956), "Religious Belief and Economic Behaviour in a Central Javanese Town" (*Economic Development and Cultural Change*, January 1956), and *The Social Context of Economic Change* (Cambridge, 1956) were followed by his major Indonesian work, *The Religion of Java* (Illinois, 1960), and two other studies, *Peddlers and Princes: Social Change and Economic Modernization in Two Indonesian Towns* (Chicago, 1963) and *Agricultural Involution* (Berkeley and Los Angeles, 1963). The whole combines to offer a series of brilliant insights into contemporary Indonesian society.

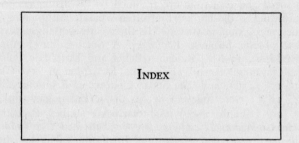

INDEX